ALEXANDER THE
GREAT

Իրաձանապէս լաղորդուեն նոյն ամեն
 եւ բանիտելից լաճլոդ, որ հայր ընտան
թեւ ասատ, անն լաղբին լաղբաեն
երեն․ Հայոց ապք հատատ հ և բիլաես տոս
անին ասատ աբեկանեն․ ապու բուն
դորգ բաղեր աստանչին պիւրեւ։

Ապատ բու գ յաղբ ոն լ ատան
ի աբեն ին յեւ տիրբինադ ․ անու
ու բո բեգ տան ենա ․ ի բանո
բու ետ բ եբ բ եբ եր բ
եր բ եբ հան բի բ անաբ
ա բ բան ատեն բին ան անս

Giampaolo
Casati

ALEXANDER THE
GREAT
the conqueror

THUNDER BAY
P·R·E·S·S

San Diego, California

ART DIRECTOR
Giorgio Seppi

MANAGING EDITOR
Tatjana Pauli

EDITING AND LAYOUTS
Studio Cancelli, Milan

COVER
Federico Magi

ENGLISH TRANSLATION
Jay Hyams

TYPESETTING
Michael Shaw

 Thunder Bay Press
An imprint of the Advantage Publishers Group
THUNDER BAY 5880 Oberlin Drive, San Diego, CA 92121-4794
P · R · E · S · S www.thunderbaybooks.com

© Mondadori Electa S.p.A., Milan

English translation © 2004 Mondadori Electa S.p.A., Milan

All notations of errors or omissions should be addressed to Thunder Bay Press, Editorial Department, at the above address. All other correspondence (author inquiries, permissions) concerning the content of this book should be addressed to Mondadori Electa S.p.A., via Trentacoste 7, 20134 Milan, Italy.

ISBN 1-59223-349-X

Library of Congress Cataloging-in-Publication Data available upon request.

Printed and bound in Spain by Artes Gráficas Toledo, SA
1 2 3 4 5 09 08 07 06 05

Contents

Preface

He became a figure of myth while still very much alive, and his death, which took him suddenly and inexplicably at only thirty-three years of age, sealed him forever in legend. Alexander the Great is one of those historical figures that remain wrapped in an aura of mystery and fascination. The story of his "earthly" existence, most of all the superhuman exploits by which, in only thirteen years, he became the most powerful ruler in the world, has been handed down to us by way of a constant stream of historical works. Achieving a critical evaluation of these works is extremely difficult, however, for they interweave fact with the purest invention. In the end one is forced to admit that the figure of the Macedonian is so complex that it eludes any unambiguous definition. Which was the "true" Alexander? The tough commander, resolute and ambitious, the ferocious warrior, or the curious traveler? The hot-tempered, vindictive monarch or the civilized, refined prince idolized by his subjects? The rational disciple of Aristotle or the fanatical mystic who believed himself the son of a god? Alexander the Great was all of these and many more. From time to time modern historians have thrown light on different aspects of his character. They have presented him as the prime example of how a single individual can change history, or as the kind of civilizing hero that justifies the ideology of colonization. Still others have made him out as the first theorist of large-scale genocide. The most recent trends call attention to the limits and serious responsibilities of Alexander's political plans. It cannot be denied that on more than one occasion Alexander used terror and even genocide to consolidate his power. However, it is equally true that his plan for his empire, based not on the domination of one race over another or one civilization over another, but rather on a mixture of cultures and faiths, was both wise and far ahead of its time. Perhaps it is precisely in that alternation of bright light and dark shadows, of glory and cruelty, that the truth about Alexander the Great should be sought.

The Kingdom of Macedonia

Philip II transformed a semibarbaric region into a great power. At his death, his son Alexander inherited not only his father's conquests but also his magnificent dream of conquering the Orient.

AT THE COURT OF PHILIP II

Alexander of Macedon, best known to moderns as Alexander the Great, was probably born in Pella, capital of the kingdom of Macedonia, either around July 20 or in October of the year 356 BC.

Biographers, writing about him long after his death, embellished the story of Alexander's life with various legendary details beginning with the omens that accompanied his birth. It was said that his father, Philip II, received word that his wife Olympias had given birth just after he had taken the city of Potidaea and that he had received two other messages that day: that his general Parmenion had defeated the Dardani, and that one of his horses had won the race at the Olympic games. Based on these three successes, soothsayers were said to have deduced that the life of the newborn would be full of triumphs. There are also those who claim that on the day of Alexander's birth, fire destroyed the great temple of Artemis at Ephesus, an event the priests interpreted as presaging future calamities for the peoples of the Orient.

In reality, at the time it occurred, Alexander's birth is not likely to have made much of an impression. He was indeed the son of the powerful and ambitious king of Macedonia, but his mother, Olympias, was only one of the king's many wives. Philip had as many as six or seven at a time, along with numerous lovers and concubines. He fathered many children with these women, including at least two other males: Arrhidaeus and Caranus. There were other possible heirs to the throne, more or less closely related to Philip.

Dynastic rules did not establish rigid rights of primogeniture. Alexander was only one of the many Macedonian princes that, in theory, might someday become king. Although the ruler had always been chosen from the family of the Argead, believed to be direct

Right: Olympias, Alexander's mother, giving birth in one of the eighty-five miniatures in the manuscript *Romance of Alexander,* made by the scribe Nersès; Armenian Mechitarist Congregation, San Lazzaro, Venice.

Below: Medallion of Olympias (obverse and reverse); Archaeological Museum, Salonika.

Opposite top: Head of Philip II made of fine-grained marble, first century AD. Some scholars believe it is a replica of a Greek original made by the sculptor Leochares; others think it is an original work.

Opposite bottom: A lake in Macedonia. During the Hellenistic period, such internal waterways were connected to the sea.

descendants of the mythical Hercules, only rarely had a firstborn son automatically succeeded his father to the throne. Far more often, the question of the succession was resolved by plots, fratricides, and usurpations.

Philip II himself, who had been the third-born son of King Amyntas III, had taken power officially as regent of his nephew (also called Amyntas), who was still the designated heir. The title of king was legally not due him, but Philip had earned it with his vitality and charisma, qualities that had won him acclaim as effective sovereign from the

assembly of the soldiers, the only group to have a say in such decisions. And since the assembly was often manipulated by the kingdom's aristocratic families, one must conclude that in Macedonia royalty was determined by the personal qualities of the aspiring ruler, along with whatever political support he could muster. As for this support, Alexander did not begin from an advantaged position. His mother, Olympias, was the daughter of the king of Epirus, Neoptolemus. She was thus a foreign princess, was known for her arrogant and passionate character, and was somewhat unpopular at court, in part because of her eccentric religious habits. In fact, the queen was active in various mystical cults and participated in orgiastic rites and Dionysian processions. In the course of these ceremonies Olympias, in the grip of Bacchic furor, behaved with the wild ardor of a maenad, even exhibiting herself dancing with giant snakes, which she was said to raise in her apartments. This adhesion to a barbaric cult, more tolerated than accepted by the cultivated and civilized citizens of Greece, could not fail but create embarrassments at Pella. For generations, the king and his courtiers had been making efforts to prove they were no longer savage and had instead become more like true Greeks, completely dedicated to only the most noble and harmonious manifestations of Hellenic spirituality.

This process of acculturation had been brought to a conclusion by Philip II, the first Macedonian king to have a complete Greek education, most of all in the military field. This was in part a result of the three years that the adolescent Philip spent as a hostage at Thebes after one of his older brothers had been defeated by that city's army.

During those years the city of Thebes, profiting from the crisis afflicting Athens and Sparta, exhausted by the long Peloponnesian War, had enjoyed a short period of domination over the other Greek cities. This had been possible in part because of its adoption of innovative military techniques, most especially the "phalanx," the formation of infantry in several rows, their long spears extended, to form a solid

Left: The *Farnese Hercules,* a marble statue by the Athenian sculptor Glycon; Museo Archeological Nazionale, Naples. This is an enlarged replica of the bronze statue made by the sculptor Lysippos, one of the masters of the fourth century BC. Hercules, or Heracles, was believed to be the mythical founder of the royal family of Macedonia.

Above: A maenad dancing with leopard and serpent, vase painting from ca. 490 BC.

Opposite: Miniature from the manuscript of *The Romance of Alexander* depicting Philip consulting the oracle at Delphi and the young Alexander taming Bucephalus.

block. The famous generals Pelopidas and Epaminondas perfected the phalanx. Gifted with brilliant intelligence and a sharp sense of observation, Philip witnessed that famous army in action and brought home to Macedonia what he learned, soon outdoing his teachers.

Although most Greeks—and not without reason—still looked on Macedonia as a somewhat backward region, it possessed several features of enormous advantage to anyone who, like Philip II, had ambitious plans for expansion. The vast plain extending between Mount Olympus and the Pindus mountain range furnished an abundant harvest of grain and favored the raising of horses; the forests of the Chalcidian peninsula, which Philip had wrested from the Athenians, provided great reserves of wood for shipbuilding. The rich gold and silver mines of Pangaeus, personal property of the king, produced all the wealth necessary to meet military needs.

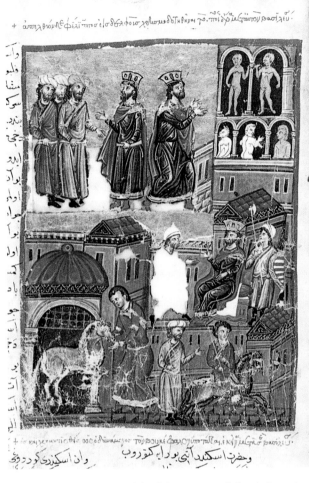

To this wealth of natural resources was added the fact that the Macedonians, forced for centuries to defend themselves against the raids of the Thracians and Illyrians, their savage neighbors, were well accustomed to the use of arms. This eliminated the need to hire mercenaries, as was the habit among almost all the cities of Greece.

All that was required was a leader to organize the ranks and lead them in battle. The opportunity presented itself in the person of Philip, who organized and trained an army capable of rivaling those of the southern cities and then set off on a series of triumphal military campaigns.

First he subdued the states, until then independent of northern Macedonia, the princes of which rushed to serve in his royal army. He then set about conquering, one by one, the independent cities along the borders of his kingdom, including those allied to Athens. On the basis of these victories, Philip managed to have himself accepted as ruler by the peoples of northern Greece, such as the Thessalians. For the first time in its history, Macedonia was no longer a conquered land but had become a power in expansion. Its ruler, however, had in mind far different plans.

The Macedonians: Greeks or Barbarians?

Settled for many centuries in the vast plains and mountainsides in the region to the north of Thessaly, the Macedonians for a long time were only a population of shepherds divided in totemic clans that practiced a form of sheep raising based on transhumance. Their ethnic origins are still unclear. Without doubt they were an Indo-European people, but they differed from the Illyrian and Thracian tribes that lived in nearby areas. In all probability they were in some way related to the populations of Hellas even if, because of their near-total isolation, the Macedonians had not been part of the cultural and civil growth in the nearby southern regions. Their language was a dialect of the Greek language, but because of the region's autonomy it had developed in an independent way, such that in historical times it was almost incomprehensible to true Greeks, also because of its very particular pronunciation, which turned *ch* into *g* and *f* in *b*, and pronounced the name of the king as "Bilip."

More than linguistic differences, what made them suspect in the eyes of the Greeks was their backwardness, making them similar to barbarian populations. Closed in their deeply forested wilderness valleys, still home to wolves and bears and still contested by warlike tribes, the Macedonians were late to develop a group consciousness. In historical times, the social, economic, and religious conditions of the country had been decidedly primitive. The inhabitants lived in small, undefended villages in the middle of the woods, and even the capitals, Aigai and Pella, completely lacked the political activities that were believed to be fundamental in all the communities of Hellas. Primordial forms of organization still held on in Macedonia. Without written laws, a man's value was measured by his skills as a hunter or a warrior against his neighbors and by his ability to drink large quantities of alcoholic drinks. At banquets, those who had not yet killed a boar or a man had to sit apart, on uncomfortable stools. The very organization of the state, based on the presence of a king, a figure that by then had disappeared almost everywhere in Greece, was so archaic that it

Gold funeral mask and bronze helmet, ca. 520 BC, found in a tomb at Sindos; Archeological Museum, Salonika. The mask is made of embossed gold leaf to which the nose, made from another leaf, was attached. The helmet is of the Illyrian type.

Opposite top: Silver octadrachm of Alexander I the Philhellene (495–442 BC), showing a horseman armed with two lances, perhaps the king himself.

Opposite bottom: Four terra-cotta heads from 480 BC found among the tombs of the sepulchers discovered between 1980 and 1982 near Sindos, about twenty-five miles west of Thessalonica. The images probably represent subterranean divinities.

recalled the ancient monarchies of Homer, with their rulers that became leaders in time of war but during peacetime hardly differed from the feudal barons that surrounded them at court. These conditions began to change beginning in the fifth century BC, when permanent relations with the southern cities were established. From then on, the members of the ruling dynasty, the Argeads, made efforts to join the Greek civilization and openly proclaimed their Greekness. The ancestor of Philip II, Alexander I, called Philhellene, "friend of the Greeks," managed to prove the Argive origin of his family, and to thus qualify for admission to the Olympic games, which were off-limits to all barbarians. His nephew Archelaus sought to transform Pella into a cultural center, generously hosting artists and writers, among them the famous dramatist Euripides. The modernization of the country was completed by Philip II, who continued and expanded the policies of Archelaus.

Above: Two of the sixty-six miniatures from *Eskandarname* by Ahmedi (mid-fifteenth century), in which the education of the son of Philip is narrated.

Below: Alexander, Philip II, and Olympias as Pan, Dionysus, and Ariadne in an ivory wall sconce found in the tomb of the prince at Vergina.

Opposite: The ruins of the ancient city of Pella.

THE EDUCATION OF A CONQUEROR

Alexander's education took place in the shadow of his father's successes. The young prince was soon removed from the loving and possessive attentions of his mother to be entrusted, while still a child, to the Epirot Leonidas. This first teacher put most of his efforts into habituating Alexander to fatigues and discomforts, educating him in an austere and rigorous way for his future life as a soldier. Leonidas was later joined by the Greek preceptor Lysimachus, who won over Alexander by filling his imagination with the story of the Trojan War and by comparing him to the hero Achilles, believed to be the founder of the family of Olympias.

Alexander's education came to involve several of his contemporaries, sons of aristocratic families

of the kingdom; the future leader made lifetime friendships with some of these boys. First among these was Hephaistion, with whom Alexander established such a tight bond of friendship that Lysimachus conferred on him the nickname Patroclus, after the close friend of Achilles.

According to his biographers, Alexander demonstrated a courageous and determined character even in his early youth. Sure proof of this was the famous episode of the horse Bucephalas. Bucephalas, it is said, was a black stallion of extraordinary beauty, but so wild and unmanageable that Philip and his attendants decided against purchasing the horse. Although only a boy, Alexander dared to criticize this decision, saying they were losing an excellent horse "for want of boldness to manage him." His father reproached him for finding fault with his

more experienced elders; when Alexander insisted he could tame the horse, Philip challenged him to prove it.

Alexander had noticed that the horse was shying at its own shadow, and he rushed to it, turned it into the sun, and leapt onto it, soon taming it. At this point, his father began to cry from both joy and pride.

From then on, Bucephalas was Alexander's battle horse, destined to accompany him on all his campaigns until, having escaped a thousand perils, he died of old age.

Whether this tale is true or false, Philip seems to have devoted much attention to his promising son and took great interest in his education. In particular, he made certain Alexander had a truly exceptional teacher: Aristotle, the most brilliant

Left: Bronze statuette of the young Alexander on horseback, made between 300 and 250 BC; Museo Nazionale di Villa Giulia, Rome.

Opposite: Bust of Aristotle of unknown provenance. The head is in Greek marble, the clothing is of alabaster; Museo Nazionale Romano.

Below: Alexander taming Bucephalus, bronze statuette from the fourth to third century BC; Museo Archeologico, Florence.

student of the famous Plato. Aristotle was probably chosen not only for his fame but also for the fact that his father had already attended the Macedonian court as a doctor. Furthermore, Aristotle was the son-in-law of Hermeias, a powerful lord of Atarneus, in Asia Minor, a fact that could play an important role in Philip's political designs in that area.

Plutarch

"Seeing him turn at the end of his career, and come back rejoicing and triumphing for what he had performed, they burst out into acclamations of applause; and his father shedding tears, it is said, for joy, kissed him as he came down from his horse and in his transport said, 'O my son, look thee out a kingdom equal to and worthy of thyself, for Macedonia is too little for thee.'"

Aristotle, at the time forty years old, arrived in Macedonia in 343 BC. The king put at his disposition a sanctuary sacred to the nymphs, immersed in the green of the winemaking region then called the Gardens of Midas. Aristotle stayed there for three years, giving lessons to Alexander and a group of royal pages his age. The youths received an excellent literary preparation. In addition to studying Homer and the great classical tragedians, their lessons also included the writings of Herodotus, the father of history writing, whose work on the Persian War was destined to have a profound influence on the future conqueror of Asia. Under the guidance of Aristotle, Alexander and his companions also studied geography and the sciences, in particular zoology and botany, subjects in which Alexander demonstrated great interest throughout his life. Aristotle also gave his students training in the field of

A Powerful War Machine

The twenty-year reign of Philip II was a period of incessant struggles during which Macedonia went from being an insignificant border state of Greece to being a hegemonic power on the peninsula. The primary instrument in this extraordinary evolution was the permanent army that Philip trained and organized in a highly efficient way, coherently blending its various units. The basic unit of the Macedonian force was the powerful cavalry,

the phalanx of the Foot Companions, soldiers with armor and long lances (sarissas, up to sixteen feet in length), trained to fight in a compact formation. Added to this body were the Shield Bearers, a mobile assault unit whose members were armed with a large shield and a shorter lance. The army was completed by archers and such artillery as catapults and ballistae, weapons that were effective even over relatively long distances.

Left: Sarissa heads from the funeral tumulus of Philip II; Archaeological Museum, Salonika.

Below: Drawing showing the phalanx in attack.

traditionally the privilege of the kingdom's young nobles, called the hetairoi, *meaning "royal companions." These horsemen, who rode with neither saddle nor stirrups (unknown in antiquity) were protected by helmets and light breastplates of leather or metal and fought with swords and long lances. Philip flanked the cavalry with strong heavy infantry,*

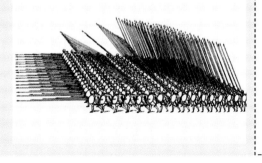

medicine, at least enough to treat wounds and prescribe cures. Naturally, a great deal of attention was given to the subject of ethics. Without doubt, Aristotle instructed his students in the importance of virtues, and Alexander translated these teachings into the desire to always excel and prove himself the best. According to biographers, Aristotle's

Above: The Parthenon, the temple dedicated to Athena Parthenos. Erected on the Acropolis of Athens between 447 and 432 BC, it was the religious center of the city.

Opposite: Alexander and his friend Hephaistion hunting deer; mosaic from Pella, Macedonia.

wide-ranging knowledge was well suited to Alexander's insatiable curiosity and he spent many happy moments in the company of the philosopher for whom he had boundless admiration.

Alexander's intellectual education did not overlook the practical. Since Arrhidaeus, Philip's only other male son, suffered a form of mental retardation (caused, according to some, by poison given him by Olympias), Philip often called the young Alexander to him to initiate him in the secrets of politics and diplomacy.

Plutarch

"*Whenever he heard Philip had taken any town of importance, or won any signal victory, instead of rejoicing at it altogether, he would tell his companions that his father would anticipate everything, and leave him and them no opportunities of performing great and illustrious actions.*"

The exercise of authority among the Macedonians was not a simple matter. Among other things, it was necessary to display one's virile skills, to be the best at hunting and also at the colossal drinking of wine, which in the north, unlike the rest of Greece, was drunk undiluted.

Also in these aspects of ruling the young prince demonstrated great promise, as is indicated by the fact that when he was only sixteen his father thought him suitable to represent him, naming him regent.

In 340 BC, when Philip set off to battle against Byzantium, Alexander assumed the functions of ruler for the first time. He received Persian ambassadors and even undertook a punitive expedition against the Thracians. From then on, he was alongside his father in every undertaking.

HEGEMONY OVER GREECE

Wielding a matchless army and backed by the financial resources to support it, Philip began to lay the basis for his supremacy over the Hellenic world. His tactics consisted of seeking to draw the various cities into his political orbit, and to do so without giving the impression of seeking to end their independence. This plan, however, ran up against the strong resistance of those Greek citizens who still nourished hegemonic dreams of their own, chief among them the Athenians. Even if heavily penalized by the unfortunate war against Sparta that had long since ended its expansion, Athens continued to maintain an undeniable authority over all the other communities. Many of its citizens wanted to see the

The Battle of Chaeronea

The battle of Chaeronea was the last heroic attempt by the Thebans and Athenians to free themselves from the political and military power of Macedonia. The battle took place in the summer of 338 BC near the Cephissus River and began with the attack of the Athenian troops arranged on the left wing of the Greek formation. The Athenian hoplites went into action before daylight and seemed to catch Philip's troops unprepared, for, following his orders, they began to withdraw. At this point the Theban phalanx and the famous Sacred Battalion, a select unit composed of warriors who had sworn to die rather than surrender, made the mistake of leaving their position on the hill to join the fight. This is what the Macedonians had been waiting for. A sudden charge of the cavalry of the Companions, led by the eighteen-year-old Alexander, surprised the enemy infantry with it ranks open because of the irregular terrain, and threw it into disarray, slaughtering them. Philip then reversed his retreat and charged with all his troops, encircling the Theban and Athenian ranks, who lost thousands of men between the dead and those taken prisoner. In a few hours the Macedonians and Thessalians had defeated the allied forces of Greece.

Above: Bronze arrowhead dating to 348 BC, year of the siege of Olynthus; the shaft bears the letters "Filippo" in relief.

Right: The monumental stone lion erected in memory of the Athenians and Thebans killed in the battle of Chaeronea, where they tried to fight off Macedonian hegemony.

city's former maritime empire brought back to life. The most forceful and determined of these nationalists was the orator Demosthenes. He was very much aware of the danger posed by the Macedonian king (whom he personally looked upon as a barbarian), and he attacked him in a series of vehement orations that came to be known as the Philippics. Demosthenes, who reproved his fellow citizens for the past inertia they had shown the ambitious monarch, succeeded in convincing the Athenians not only to take up arms but also to make alliances with other cities, including their ancient rival, Thebes. Putting aside their pride, they even accepted Theban military leadership. Faced with the threat of losing their age-old independence, most of the Greeks joined to form a compact anti-Macedonian front. The final encounter was inevitable, but when the old armies of hoplites found themselves facing the more mobile and modern Macedonian army with its indomitable cavalry, the outcome was not long in doubt. The decisive battle took place on the plain of Chaeronea, in August of 338 BC. The Thebans discovered that their arms were no longer invincible and that the legendary courage of the Theban Sacred Battalion had little value against the assault of the cavalry led by the eighteen-year-old Alexander. At the end of the day Philip succeeded at doing what none of the great powers of Greece and not even the monstrous Persian Empire had been able to achieve: win clear and complete

Philip of Macedonia assembling his army to battle Darius; this miniature from a fifteenth-century Turkish manuscript is among the few images from Muslim literature that refer to the infancy of Alexander and the deeds of Philip.

Plutarch

"He was fair and of a light color, passing into ruddiness in his face and upon his breast. Aristoxenus tells us that a most agreeable odor exhaled from his skin and that his breath and body all over was so fragrant as to perfume the clothes he wore."

rule over the Greek peninsula. Now that he was ruler of the field, however, the Macedonian king had to conquer Greece with the arms of diplomacy, proving that he was not an oppressor but rather the defender of a common peace. This he achieved through the creation of a new organization of states that took its name from the city in which it was founded: the League of Corinth. The league, which included all the cities except Sparta, which held itself apart, served primarily military purposes, both offensive and defensive. It also had a federal assembly in which each of the confederated cities had a number of representatives in proportion to the size of the

Above: Two projectiles for slings made of lead and bearing, in relief, an abbreviation of the name Philip II. These were found amid the ruins of Olynthus, a city besieged by Philip. The sling was primarily a nuisance weapon, often used by armies in antiquity.

Opposite top: Gold head of Medusa in the form of a wall sconce that was located in the antechamber of the tomb of Philip at Vergina, intended to frighten visitors.

Opposite bottom: Vergina, floor mosaic and ruins of the royal palace.

were now destined to gravitate within the sphere of Macedonian influence. In fact, Philip immediately assured himself of his supremacy over the entire peninsula, throwing out all hostile governments and setting up in their place ones loyal to him. He established garrisons in strategic areas, even putting a Macedonian garrison in Thebes itself to maintain control of the city. Philip treated Athens with special generosity, but even this served his plans. The capital of Attica, cradle of Greek civilization, aside from enjoying indisputable prestige among all those who, like the Macedonians, declared themselves Greek, still possessed Greece's most powerful fleet, an essential tool in Philip's plans. For these reasons, Philip made no demands of reparations from Athens and instead made a display of his benevolence, sending the city a high-profile friendly delegation composed of his son Alexander and his old councillor Antipater, to whom he had entrusted the task of bringing home the ashes of the Athenians fallen in battle. Evidently Alexander, who had already won himself fame as a warrior and battle leader at the battle of Chaeronea, was by now considered by his father a valid and trusted collaborator. In all probability, the ambitious Philip was preparing his son for new, important responsibilities in the project he had been planning for a long time, a project worthy of the greatness of its designer. Having eliminated all opposition in Greece, political or military, Philip felt free to undertake the realization of the dream that the cities of Hellas had nourished for generations: to march against the Persian Empire and defeat it on the field of battle.

The rivalry between Greeks and Persians dated back to the period of the war between the two peoples fought between 500 and 479 BC. The struggle had ended with the Athenian victories at Salamis and Plataea, which had won the independence of Hellas.

military contingent it furnished the alliance. The independence of the various members was thus nominally guaranteed, and the Macedonians were not even represented in the assembly, but Philip served as commander-for-life of the league's army and was the arbiter and guarantor of its harmony. In reality, despite all assurances to the contrary, the Macedonian king used the treaty to seal the end of the independence of the Greek cities, all of which

But in the collective consciousness of the Greeks, the desire to avenge the destruction suffered remained very much alive, together with the desire to free the Greek cities of Asia Minor that were subject to the empire. Since the end of the Persian War there had been peace between the empire and the Greek cities, even though it was in truth an armed peace, sometimes interrupted by raids and military expeditions by cities like Sparta and Athens, which on several occasions had sent mercenary troops to assist officials or princes rebelling against Persian power. For their part, the Persian kings had never ceased their involvement in the internal affairs of Greece. For more than a century, the kings of Persia had provided assistance to one or another of the Greek cities in order to prevent the formation of a dangerous hegemony. At the time of Philip, the so-called King's Peace was still in force. This treaty served to maintain the situation of balance, a substantial benefit to the Persians. For several years the Persians had been following with apprehension the growth of Macedonian power, and efforts had been made to contain it, instigating the southern cities against it. The orator Demosthenes, for example, and been amply subsidized by the Persian kings. For some time, however, the situation on the Persian side of the Aegean Sea had been presenting difficulties of its own. There had been a great revolt of the satraps, the governors of the imperial provinces, and the last two rulers, Artaxerxes

Greeks and Persians

The history of the relationship between the Persians and the Greeks is composed primarily of armed conflict over control of the Aegean Sea and the eastern Mediterranean. The rivalry began in 500 BC when the Greek cities of Ionia, annexed to the Persian Empire, tried without luck to rebel against the Persians. Since Athens had helped the rebels, Darius I decided to punish the city and sent to Greece an enormous expedition that was defeated in 490 BC by the Athenian general Miltiades in the battle of Marathon. A few years later, in 480 BC, Xerxes, son of Darius, sought to avenge his father. To this end he assembled an even larger army and again invaded Greece. This time the invaders were faced by the armies of various cities joined in an alliance. Despite the heroic resistance of the Spartans led by Leonidas at Thermopylae, the Persians occupied and sacked Athens. Their victory was brief. Having taken refuge on the nearby islands, the Athenians reorganized in a short time and, led by Themistocles, destroyed the Persian fleet in the battle of Salamis. The next year the same fate touched the Persian army, which was destroyed in the battle of Platea. Greece thus preserved its independence and political freedom, indispensable conditions for the development of its culture and civilization.

Corinthian warrior in bronze from ca. 500 BC, found at Dodona.

III Ochus and his son, had been assassinated by a court eunuch, events followed by periods of trouble.

The right time for Philip II's plan seemed to have arrived. In the spring of 337 BC the Macedonian king easily convinced the assembly of the League of Corinth to declare war. The initial phase of the expedition began the next summer. Because Persian agents had captured and executed Hermeias of Atarneus, an ally of the Macedonians, Philip sent a small expedition to Asia Minor commanded by the generals Attalus and Parmenion with orders to establish a bridgehead. He himself was planning to follow soon after at the head of the bulk of the army, but destiny decided otherwise.

THE DEATH OF A KING

A dangerous situation had been taking shape at the Macedonian royal court for a period of several months. It began around the time of the declaration of war, when Philip, forty-five years old, decided to get married again. In and of itself this was not at all noteworthy. To guarantee his succession, a Macedonian ruler had to create a large number of descendants. There was also the fact that his favorite son, Alexander, was certain to face considerable risks in the military campaign about to begin. What aroused attention was the fact that the new queen, unlike Philip's other wives, who by then were too

old to bear new heirs, was Macedonian and belonged to one of the most powerful clans in the kingdom. In fact, the chosen bride was the very young Cleopatra, niece of Attalus, one of the most eminent

Left: Gold earrings of elegant workmanship from an Archaic-period tomb at Vergina.

Above: A "reclining couple" on the cover of a marble sarcophagus from the fourth century BC.

Opposite top: View of the Macedonian plain from the heights of Philippi.

Left: Map showing the locations of Macedonia, facing the Aegean Sea, between Thrace and Thessaly.

Below: Small ivory portrait head of Philip II, from Vergina, the ancient Aigai, where Alexander's father was murdered during the wedding celebration for a daughter. His tomb, found unplundered in 1977 by Manolis Andronicos under an artificial tumulus about forty feet high, contained invaluable testimony of the Macedonian civilization.

Opposite: Alexander wearing the aegis in a statue from the Hellenistic period; Fitzwilliam Museum, Cambridge (Massachusetts).

men at court. A son born to this new couple would be Macedonian on both sides, father and mother, and would thus be looked upon with great favor by the more traditionalist Macedonians, certainly with greater favor than that accorded the son of the unruly Epirot princess Olympias. It also seems that during the nuptial banquet Attalus, showing a glaring lack of tact, had toasted the future birth of "a legitimate heir," thus attracting the furious reaction of the hot-tempered Alexander, who saw himself demoted from the standing of heir to that of illegitimate son. It seems that only Philip's intervention had prevented the young man from killing the elderly general. But an incurable wound had been opened in the family. Until then Olympias, as the mother of the hereditary prince, had enjoyed a privileged position among the wives. Enraged, she left court to take refuge in her birthplace, where she tried to get her relatives to go to war against Philip. Alexander went with her, made certain she was welcomed with all honors, and at the same time probably did his best to calm her. The next year, thanks to the intervention of a Greek diplomat, the father and son reached at least a formal reconciliation, but their relationship remained tense, also because Cleopatra had meanwhile given birth to two children, one of them male. Feeling increasingly insecure in his position, Alexander tried to win back prestige by arbitrarily inserting himself in some of his father's diplomatic negotiations. Philip had been trying to arrange a marriage between Arrhidaeus and the daughter of Pixodarus, a powerful satrap of Caria, with whom Philip hoped to form an alliance. By way of friends, Alexander proposed to take the place of his half-brother, boasting that he would make a far better match than the "half-witted" Arrhidaeus. When Philip learned of this, he turned furiously on his son, humiliating him in front of his friends. Was it possible that the presumed heir to the kingdom of Macedonia would debase himself so much as to marry the daughter of a servant of a foreign king? This may have been an effective lesson in diplomacy, but it did little to improve relations between father and son. The negotiations ended without a marriage, and Philip banished all of Alexander's friends who had been involved in the affair. The humiliated Alexander had to submit to his father's decisions, but one can assume that from then on the authority and even the presence of his father became increasingly insupportable to him.

Shortly after the conclusion of this affair, Philip tried to reconcile himself with the court of Epirus by giving one of his daughters in marriage to Olympias's brother. In the course of the magnificent marriage celebration, however, just as the king, preceded by statues of the twelve Greek gods, was about to make his triumphal entry to the theater of Aigai, the ancient capital of the kingdom, a bodyguard named Pausanias stabbed him to death. Thus died, at forty-seven years of age and on the threshold of his great undertaking, the man who had brought Greece into a new era.

According to some versions, Pausanias confessed that he decided to commit the act when he realized

Right: Gold bow-case and greaves, protection for the shins, two pieces of the armor of King Philip as it was found on the site at Vergina.

Below: Gold crown of myrtle that was deposited on the charred bones. Of highly delicate artistry, it is the heaviest of those from classical antiquity to have survived.

Opposite top: Reverse of a tetradrahm of Alexander the Great with Zeus enthroned and the inscription "Basileos Alexandrou."

that the king had no intention of taking his side against Attalus, who had gravely offended him. His declaration did not quell the suspicions that the true instigators of the murder were Olympias and Alexander. Aside from her notoriously bad temper, Olympias had a motive for the murder, but she also had an alibi. She had been far away, in Epirus, at the moment of the crime and could not easily have directed the plot. As for Alexander, he had seen his hopes of inheriting his father's kingdom vacillate and thus had a motive for killing Philip, and had been present at the scene. He certainly possessed the resolve and ruthlessness for such an undertaking. In addition, for quite a while Olympias had been telling him that he was not really the son

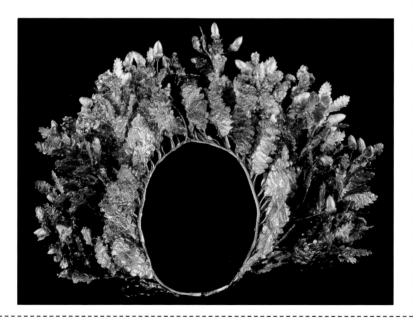

of Philip but rather of a divinity that had miraculously conceived him in the form of lightning or a serpent. Believing that would certainly have eliminated a great many scruples. On the other hand, Alexander would have known that this was not the best time for him to lay claim to the succession. Without doubt, his chances would have been greater if, for example, he had waited to earn even greater military fame in Asia. It should also be said that such a murder seems out of character for Alexander, given his lifelong aversion to all forms of treason or duplicity. In any case, from a distance of more than two thousand years the crime must remain unsolved. Our sources, even the most

reliable, simply do not offer enough to build on, for which reason we must suspend judgment.

ALEXANDER, KING OF MACEDONIA

Following his father's death, circumstances forced Alexander to act quickly. Laying claim to the succession was clearly not going to be easy. The soldiers were used to the strong, dominating character of Philip; they were familiar with the habits of the big, bearded man, with his disfigured face and body covered with the scars of wounds received in battle. Would they accept in his place a boy barely twenty years old, with hairless cheeks and an almost

The Royal Tombs of Vergina

Events that occurred in 1977 on the site of Vergina can be considered the most important archaeological find in Macedonia. In the course of excavations led by the Greek archaeologist Manolis Andronicos, three tombs dating to the period of Alexander were brought to light, two of them miraculously intact. The find confirmed the identification of modern Vergina as Aigai, the ancient ceremonial capital of the Macedonian rulers. Artifacts of extraordinary importance were found in the excavations, including a gold casket weighing ten kilograms, decorated with an eight-pointed star, that contained the cremated remains of a man about forty years old who had died around the middle of the fourth century BC. It was clearly the burial of a ruler, and, since Alexander had been buried in Egypt, most historians concluded that this had to be the tomb of Philip II. Other scholars hold that it is instead the tomb of Arrhidaeus, the half-brother and successor of Alexander. The site of Vergina, with its vivid frescoes and invaluable artifacts, including a helmet and set of greaves currently displayed in the archaeological museum of Salonika, constitutes one of the main sources of information about the civilization that gave rise to the conquests of Alexander the Great.

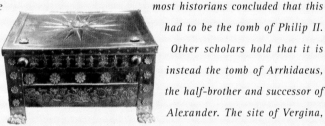

Solid-gold funerary box with lion's-paw feet, from the tomb of Philip II at Vergina; Archaeological Museum, Salonika.

feminine beauty? Would the powerful Macedonian aristocracy look favorably on the son of a foreigner? Weren't they far more likely to favor the son of Cleopatra, niece of Attalus? To Alexander's good fortune, Attalus was far away in Asia, so from that point of view the road was open. There were other claimants to the throne, but Alexander and Olympias, who on news of her husband's death had immediately rushed back to Macedonia, did not leave them room in which to maneuver.

Having obtained the support of Antipater, with whom he had gone on the mission to Athens, and probably also that of Parmenion, his father's right arm, Alexander behaved as though there was no question of his right to the throne. He began by seeing to his father's funeral, having him cremated and buried in a suitable manner at Aigai;

he then gave orders to investigate the murder. Two princes that could lay claim to the throne were immediately accused of having been the instigators of the murder and were put to death. A little later Alexander's cousin Amyntas, for whom Philip had been regent, was executed. Olympias took revenge on her rivals, having the children of Philip's last marriage massacred and forcing Cleopatra to commit suicide. At that point it became clear that Attalus too had to be eliminated, so amid the more or less total indifference of his friends and relatives he was killed. Of all the possible pretenders to the throne only Arrhidaeus, Alexander's mentally retarded half-brother, was spared, probably because his condition made him an unlikely contender. At the conclusion of this show of force Alexander had

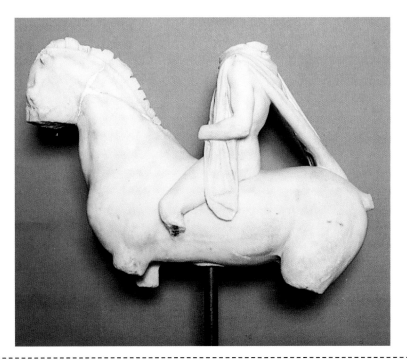

Above: Head of Alexander found in 1886 near the Erechtheum of Athens.

Left: Statuette of a young Macedonian horseman wearing the chlamys, the short mantle of military use. The work, found at Pella, is believed to be from the late Hellenistic period and is dated to around the middle of the fourth century BC.

Opposite top: Ruins of Corinth, where the Panhellenic congress began meeting in 338 BC.

Opposite bottom: Silver alabastron found at Vergina in the tomb of Philip II. It bears two heads in relief, one of Hercules (shown), the other of Alexander.

no difficulty obtaining official recognition from the army. Urged on by Antipater, Philip's veterans joined in assembly and acclaimed the new ruler in accordance with their ancient traditions. Even the Macedonian aristocrats, those from whom Alexander had expected the greatest resistance, accepted this fait accompli. Alexander had adroitly convinced them that the monarchy had changed in name only and that their privileges would remain intact. Things were quite different outside the borders of the kingdom. Both to the north, among the Illyrians and the Thracians, and to the south in Greece, news of Philip II's death had the subject peoples and cities hoping to regain their independence. In Athens, Demosthenes had no difficulty convincing his fellow citizens that the successor to Philip was merely a weak boy who constituted no threat. Even Philip's oldest allies in the region,

the Thessalians, renounced their treaties of alliance and blocked the passes connecting their country to Macedonia. Alexander reacted with speed and determination. He had his sappers open a road through a mountainous region believed impassable and suddenly appeared in the rear of the Thessalians. Taken by surprise, they rushed to accept him as archon, also putting their excellent cavalry at his disposition. Alexander later dealt with the rest of the peninsula, in a short time reestablishing Macedonian rule. The young king was confirmed as leader of the League of Corinth, with all his father's prerogatives, including the mandate for the expedition to Asia. He received the homage of all the cities, including Athens, where the embittered Demosthenes saw his hopes dashed once again. According to accounts handed down by his biographers, in all of Greece only one man treated Alexander differently: Diogenes, founder of the Cynic school of philosophy. Diogenes was a singular man; having decided to renounce all worldly goods he was living at the time in an old wooden tub. Alexander sought him out and asked him if there was anything he could do for him, probably expecting the eccentric mendicant to make some outlandish request. The philosopher replied that in fact there was something he could do and asked him to move aside a little, for he was blocking the sun. According to the biographers, Alexander accepted this with good spirit, stating: "If I had not been Alexander, I would like to have been Diogenes." As difficult as we may find that to believe, this famous anecdote is one of the episodes that most struck the imagination of historians, thinkers, and artists and throws a bright light on both its protagonists.

Having settled for the time being the situation in the south, Alexander hastened north, where the barbarian rulers believed themselves freed of the yoke Philip had imposed on them. Alexander's first objective was the proud tribe of the Triballians, a Thracian population that directly threatened the borders of his kingdom. Leaving Antipater in the capital, Alexander marched against this enemy at the head of a large army that was supported by a small fleet of warships, which was given the task of ascending the Ister River (today's Danube). For the first time Alexander was acting on his own, without the assistance of any of his father's trusted councillors, and he proved himself perfectly capable

Left: High-relief marble sculpture by Pierre Puget (1620–1694) depicting the encounter between Alexander the Great and Diogenes; Louvre, Paris.

Right: Silver gilt panel of a Thracian horseman armed with a lance, with a horse's head behind him.

Below: Chalcedony cameo from a late epoch with the bust of Alexander in profile.

of handling the complex war machine his father had created. Alexander's first task was to break enemy resistance in the mountainous region of the central Balkans. The Triballians had barricaded a narrow gorge with a line of carts in front of them that served both defensive and offensive uses, since they could be rolled downhill. Having determined that the position could not be attacked from its flanks, Alexander sent his men forward. When the Triballians rolled the carts toward them, he instructed his soldiers to either open their ranks or throw themselves to the ground and use their large shields for protection. Following Alexander's command, they took the position without losses. But the war was not over. The Triballians took refuge in forests, but Alexander drove them out using his slingers and archers, and then attacked them with his infantry and cavalry. He drove the Triballians back to the Ister, where their king and his most loyal followers took refuge on an island, protected on the riverbanks by mounted troops. Since the warships that had ascended the river were too few to permit an all-out attack, Alexander had his men build rafts by stuffing their tent skins with hay. In this way the Macedonians made it across the Ister. The crossing took place in the middle of the night, and in the morning the Macedonians were able to make a surprise attack with all their forces, obtaining the surrender of the enemy. From then on the Triballians and the other Thracian tribes submitted to Alexander's authority and later participated as his allies in the expedition to Asia. From the very beginning of the campaign

difficult situations. A few weeks after the campaign against the Thracians, the Macedonian soldiers had to battle the Illyrians and the Taulanti in the swampy regions along the western borders of Macedonia. These were warlike and indomitable warriors, and Alexander had great difficulty in subduing them. During the siege of the king of the Illyrians in the stronghold of Pellium, Alexander found himself attacked in turn by the Taulanti. By means of an audacious maneuver involving a dangerous bluff, he succeeded in breaking the encirclement and was victorious in a large battle that took place in the late summer of 335 BC. He was prevented from fully exploiting this success because unwelcome news arrived almost immediately. In Greece, the rumor was spreading that Alexander had been killed in battle and the Macedonian kingdom was in danger. Thebans had attacked the garrison established by Philip in their city, while Athens, urged on as usual by Demosthenes and financed by the Persians, was rearming. Alexander lost no time. With one of the forced marches destined to astonish his enemies, he reached central Greece in only thirteen days. He arrived outside the walls of Thebes and called for the surrender of the city. The Thebans, preparing for a long siege, refused. Alexander then attacked the walls and, it seems, noticed a postern gate in the wall that the Thebans had left unguarded. He sent his officer Perdiccas at the head of select troops to seize it, and in this way the defenses were overcome. It was a bloody struggle, with the death of more

Alexander had been promised support and a friendly alliance from another people, the Agrianians, a mountain tribe that lived near Macedonia's northern border. Their soldiers were armed with javelins, fought courageously, and were particularly adept at raids and surprise attacks. These warriors, led by their king, also followed Alexander in his undertaking and played decisive roles in many

Plutarch

"He immediately marched through the pass of Thermopylae, saying that to Demosthenes, who had called him a child while he was in Illyria and in the country of the Triballians, and a youth when he was in Thessaly, he would appear a man before the walls of Athens."

than six thousand Thebans, but the true tragedy came later. Alexander had astutely arranged for the fate of the rebels to be decided by representatives of the Greek cities that were rivals of Thebes, and they behaved in a cruel and vindictive way. The city was razed to the ground and more than thirty thousand Thebans were sold as slaves. On the orders of Alexander the only people spared were priests, friends of the Macedonians, and the descendants of the poet Pindar, who a century and a half earlier had composed poems in honor of the Macedonians. The conquest of Thebes is the subject of an anecdote involving an

act of clemency that somewhat balances the ferocity shown by Alexander. At the end of the siege, a woman was brought before him, accused of having killed the leader of a group of his Thracian allies. The prisoner, named Timoclea, was the sister of the general Theagenes, killed at Chaeronea. Standing before Alexander, the woman said that she had killed the man because he had raped her. Alexander, who according to all his biographers always treated women with respect, ordered that the fearless Timoclea and her children be set free.

The situation at Thebes was resolved, but Alexander still had to make decisions concerning Athens and all the cities that had sympathized with the rebels. Since none of them had had time to participate actively in the uprising and since many of them, including even Athens, had rushed to congratulate him on his victory, Alexander made the diplomatic decision of taking no severe reprisals. Once again the city of Athens, which had been the principal promoter of the revolt, succeeded in saving itself. Its citizens, however, had understood that the situation was now in favor of the Macedonians; thus, from that moment on they were careful not to openly challenge Alexander. For his part, Alexander had obtained what he wanted. Both the severity shown Thebes and the moderation he later displayed earned Alexander admiration and respect from the entire Greek world. Now, after removing all doubts of his abilities from the Thracians, Illyrians, and most of all the Greeks, it remained for him to take on his most difficult challenge: the expedition to Asia.

In that case, too, he was forced to act rapidly. The small expedition led by Parmenion had been defeated at Magnesia, on the Maeander River, by a Persian army led by the Greek mercenary Memnon. If help were not sent soon, the Macedonians stood to lose their bridgehead on the far side of the Aegean.

Preparations went ahead through the winter of 335–334 BC. Leaving Antipater as his lieutenant in Macedonia with enough troops to maintain control of the European territory, Alexander assembled an army of about 38,000 men. The backbone of the force was the Macedonians, more than 14,000 men, including 1,200 mounted Companions, divided into four squadrons, 9,000 foot Companions, and 3,000 Shield Bearers.

Along with these troops were contingents from Greek allies, 1,200 Thessalian horsemen, a few hundred Thracian and Paeonian explorers, and about 6,000 more composed of Agrianians, Illyrians, and other Balkan peoples. In addition to the soldiers there were also sappers and the technicians needed to make and use artillery and siege machines, secretaries, mapmakers, cooks, and quartermasters, as well as doctors, scientists, artists, and soothsayers. During the expedition this variegated mass would also have the task of seeing to the regular functioning of the administration and court.

With this army—in truth not at all enormous— Alexander intended to defeat the largest empire the Greeks had ever heard of.

Left: Fresco from the tomb of Lyson and Kallikles at Leucadia, in Macedonia, showing the typical weapons of a Macedonian warrior: round shield, swords, helmets, and greaves.

Opposite top: Map of the Achaemenid empire at the time of Darius I.

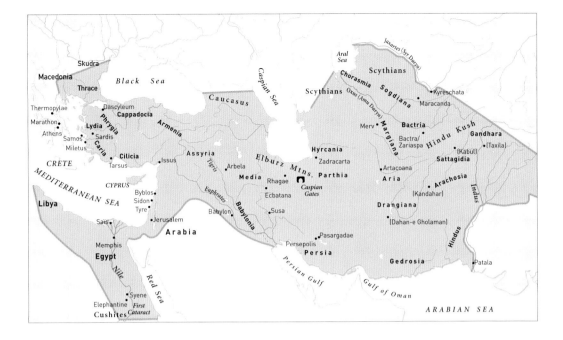

An Enormous but Fragile Empire

At the time of Philip II, the Persian Empire was an enormous territorial reality that extended over nearly 2,500 miles, from Egypt to the Indus River. It was composed of highly different regions: the fertile valley of the Nile and Mesopotamia and the sandy deserts of Libya and the Iranian plateau, the coasts of the Mediterranean and the mountains of the Hindu Kush and Caucasus. The state was divided administratively into roughly twenty satrapies, whose capitals were located along royal roads, creating an efficient road network that ensured rapid communications. Although many of these territories had been conquered as much as two centuries earlier, the unity of the empire depended on the presence of Persian officials. The subject peoples continued to speak their languages and to practice their religions, sometimes harboring dreams of independence and ready to burst into open rebellion. The symbol of the Persian empire's unity was the Great King, to whom all the populations paid tribute and homage, annually sending representatives to the royal palace at Persepolis. Following their victories in the fifth-century wars, the Greeks were no longer quite so intimidated by the Persians. Despite the Persians' financial resources and their ability to mobilize and field enormous armies, the Greeks had long begun thinking it would be possible to make the empire collapse.

Detail of reliefs on the eastern stairs of the Apadana Palace, Persepolis.

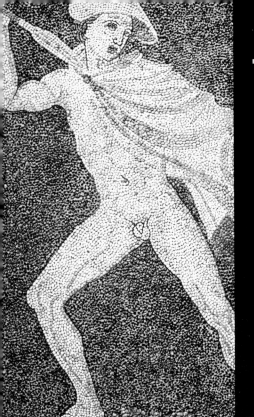

The Expedition

A ruler barely twenty years old leads a few thousand men in an undertaking without precedent: the invasion of a vast empire that can field incalculable masses of warriors.

FIRST CLASHES

The invasion of Asia began in the spring of 334 BC. Alexander was accompanied by several older associates of Philip, such as Antigonus, in command of the Greek allies, and Parmenion, who had led the first wave. Along with Alexander were several friends his own age, including those with whom he had attended the school of Aristotle: Hephaistion, Nearchus, Craterus, Ptolemy, Seleucus, and Perdiccas. Parmenion's son Philotas had command of the Companion cavalry, and Cleitus, brother of Alexander's wet nurse, led the prestigious royal squadron. The army included a large number of noncombatants, among them the treasurer Harpalus, the secretary Eumenes, the soothsayer Aristander, and the historian Callisthenes, Aristotle's cousin, who came along to write a record of the expedition.

Taking leave of her son—whom she would never see again—Olympias reminded him of the "divine mystery" of his birth. Alexander left his capital without regrets and without taking any of the precautions urged on him by his courtiers. Most of all, he refused to marry and generate an heir for the throne before setting off, which would have been prudent for the sake of the dynasty in view of the great dangers he was about to face. Instead, he made a public display of his generosity and of his determination to leave everything behind, giving most of his possessions to his friends and supporters. Perdiccas, the officer who had led the attack at Thebes, asked him what he was leaving for himself, to which he replied, "My hopes."

The army crossed Thrace, traveling in the opposite direction along the route used by the Persians in their invasions of Greece, and assembled

Plutarch

"He was naturally a great lover of all kinds of learning and reading . . . he constantly laid Homer's Iliad, *in a copy corrected by Aristotle, with his dagger under his pillow, declaring that he esteemed it a perfect portable treasure of military virtue and knowledge."*

Left: *Alexander the Great at the Tomb of Achilles*, oil on canvas by the neoclassical painter Robert Hubert (1733–1808); Louvre, Paris.

Below: Gold repoussé phiale from Iran; Museo Nazionale d'Arte Orientale, Rome.

Opposite top: Bronze equestrian statuette of Alexander from excavations at Herculaneum.

Opposite bottom: The army of Philip II of Macedon battling the troops of Darius III in a miniature from a fifteenth-century Turkish manuscript.

at the Dardanelles, where 160 Greek warships were awaiting them. Entrusting to Parmenion the task of organizing the transport, Alexander took the helm of the royal trireme and set off for Asia Minor. Halfway across, he performed propitiatory rites for the undertaking, sacrificing a bull to the sea god Poseidon and pouring out libations to the Nereids. As the ship came ashore on the coast of Asia, he hurled his spear into the soil of the Persian Empire, proclaiming his right to conquer it. This symbolic gesture also revealed his true intentions. Officially, he was leading a punitive expedition sent to vindicate the damages and destruction wrought by the armies of Darius and Xerxes and to limit Persian influence on Hellas. With this gesture, however, Alexander here gave the first hint of his true ambitions, which went far beyond what could have been imagined by even the most visionary of his companions.

Another exquisitely literary element entered into play in that moment and had a powerful effect on the young leader's imagination. Everything in the region where they landed evoked the mythical events narrated by Homer. The ships that had brought the Achaeans to that shore on their expedition to win back Helen and destroy Troy had beached along that very shoreline, and the ringing

Alexander and Homer

Although Alexander proved many times that he had a perfectly rational mind, the ancient myths, as many scholars have noted, also had an enormous influence on him. He lived immersed in the world of gods and heroes evoked by the poet Homer. Of course, the reading of the Iliad and Odyssey was a fundamental element in the instruction of every young Greek of the learned classes, and many soldiers in the Macedonian army knew by heart long sections of Homer. But for Alexander, the Iliad was far more, deeply inspiring his imagination and his faith while presenting a clear code of conduct. He had a special copy of the Homeric text, with commentary by Aristotle, and he treated it as his most valued possession, held in the most precious of the jeweled caskets taken from the enemy. On the basis of an elaborately worked out genealogy, Alexander considered Achilles his ancestor, and he took the young and passionate hero as someone to emulate and as a model against which to judge himself. The legendary warrior and great conqueror did in fact share the same destiny, that of living a glorious but very brief life.

Above: Portrait bust of Homer; Vatican Museums, Rome.

Below: *The Apotheosis of Homer*, painted by Jean-Auguste-Dominique Ingres between 1826 and 1827; Louvre, Paris.

a pilgrimage to the sites where Achilles had found glory and death. He placed a garland on the great hero's tomb and in tribute ran around it naked and anointed with oil, in the custom of athletes. His friend Hephaistion did the same at the tomb of Patroclus, Achilles' closest friend. The last stop was the temple of Athena at Troy. There Alexander offered sacrifices and dedicated his armor to the goddess; in return the priests gave him precious relics of the mythical war, including an ancient decorated shield that he was to carry with him on all his campaigns. Only at the conclusion of these evocative rituals, which served to create a connection between the world of myth and the reality he was living, did Alexander rejoin his army.

battles related in the *Iliad* had taken place on the surrounding plain. The Macedonian king, who believed himself the heir and successor of those ancient warriors, began his adventure by making

Among the members of the expeditionary force, the situation was beginning to awaken concern. Alexander's parting gifts and the costs of the

Above: Attic black-figure amphora from the sixth century BC with decoration showing Ajax bearing to safety the body of Patroclus with the weapons of Achilles.

Right: Archers of the Persian king Darius, glazed-brick wall decoration from the palace at Susa, fifth century BC.

preceding campaigns had seriously drained the royal coffers, and half of their provisions had already been consumed. New supplies had to be procured through conquest or the use of spoils. Their salvation depended on the speed with which Alexander could take hold of the Persian Empire's central territories with their fabled treasure.

The Persians had no intention of passively allowing these invaders to take the initiative.

Following a period of confusion and betrayals, a new and energetic ruler had taken the throne at Persepolis: Darius III Codomannus, a member of a secondary branch of the Achaemenid dynasty. Darius, whose power seemed far more consolidated than that of his immediate predecessors, had no intention of ceding his boundless empire without a fight and was already taking countermeasures. Although the Persian king's fleet, more powerful than Alexander's, had failed to intercept the invaders, the Persian generals began assembling their forces to drive the Greeks into the sea. But among the commanders there was no agreement on the best way to confront the situation. Before Alexander's arrival, the man who had led the Persian army with the most success was Memnon of Rhodes, a Greek in the service of the Persians. Familiar with the strengths of Macedonian troops, he proposed a tactic of containment. He suggested a scorched-earth policy, burning the crops and supplies in the path of Alexander's army to block his advance. The bellicose local satraps, who considered themselves the defenders of the imperial

Right: Obverse and reverse of a gold daric showing the Persian king as a war leader, holding a lance and bow.

Opposite above: Hilt of an Achaemenid parade sword; Archaeological Museum, Teheran.

Below: The Great King with two servants, one holding a fly whisk and the other a parasol; bas-relief decoration of a door in the palace of Persepolis, Iran.

Opposite bottom: *Alexander Crossing the Granicus*, etching by Antonio Tempesta, 1608.

Plutarch

"He fights in the front rank, at the head of his troops, riding Bucephalus. He is easily known by his buckler and a large plume of white feathers on each side of his helmet."

provinces, rejected this plan. They insisted on engaging the enemy in a pitched battle, and so sure were they of winning an easy victory that they convinced Darius that it was not necessary for him to call for a general mobilization. As a foreigner—and a Greek, the very nationality of the invaders—Memnon ran the risk of being suspected of treason, so he was forced to accept the decision to fight. The battle took place early in May in 334 BC along the Granicus River, where the contingents of the satrapies of Asia Minor had taken up positions on the steep right bank to await the arrival of the Greeks. In this instance, for the only time in the entire campaign, the Greeks enjoyed numerical superiority; the Persians had a clear advantage in terms of position. Things were further aggravated for the Greeks by the fact that they reached the field of battle late in the afternoon. Even so, Alexander rejected Parmenion's advice to make camp and attack in the morning. Boldly led by their young king, who fearlessly exposed himself

to all dangers, the Macedonian troops won their first victory.

Alexander emphasized the Panhellenic nature of the event by having all the Greek mercenaries found in the Persian army massacred, considering them traitors to the common cause. The few survivors were sent into forced labor in the mines of Thrace and Macedonia. Alexander also marked his triumph in a tangible way by sending three hundred suits of Persian armor to the Parthenon on the Acropolis of Athens. The gift was accompanied by a dedication: "Alexander son of Philip and the Greeks, except the Spartans, from the barbarians who live in Asia." It was a glory shared by all the inhabitants of Hellas, with the exception of the contemptuous Spartans, who had not participated in any way in the war. The first step of the war of revenge had been taken, and also well publicized.

With the victory on the Granicus, the first line of Persian defense had been broken. The road

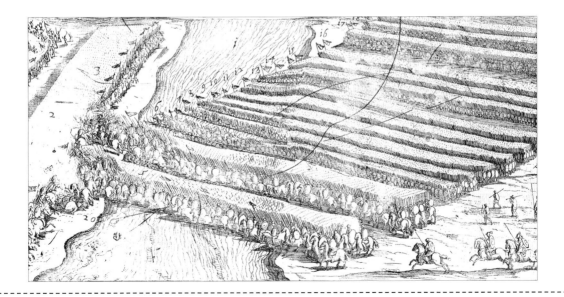

The Battle of the Granicus

In the attempt to block the Greek invasion, the Persian satraps Spithridates, Arsites, and Mithridates, rejecting Memnon's plan, chose to engage the Greeks in a major battle and took up positions on the right bank of the Granicus River. It was spring and the river, located along the main road leading inland, was running full. In their front line the Persians put their powerful cavalry. The almost 20,000 men, most wearing heavy armor, were divided into the units of the various satrapies. Behind them, on the rocky ridge overlooking the plain, were the Greek mercenaries. When he arrived on the field, Alexander immediately took up a position on the opposite bank and lined up his troops to form a longer front than that of the Persians. On the right wing, which he personally commanded, he placed the Agrianian assault troops and the Macedonian and Paeonian cavalry; in the center went the phalanx and the Shield Bearers; on the left, under command of Parmenion, were the Greek and Thessalian cavalry.

Since the steep, muddy banks ruled out a large-scale frontal attack, Alexander decided to make use of a diversion. He ordered one of the squadrons of

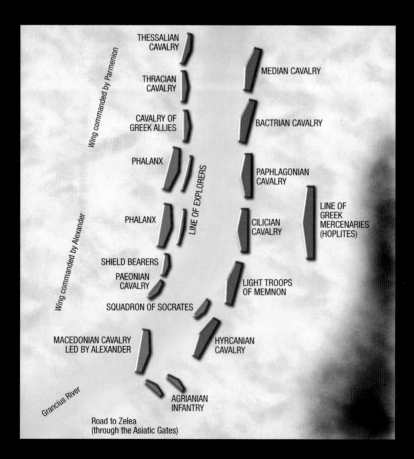

THESSALIAN CAVALRY

Wing commanded by Parmenion

THRACIAN CAVALRY

CAVALRY OF GREEK ALLIES

PHALANX

PHALANX

SHIELD BEARERS

PAEONIAN CAVALRY

SQUADRON OF SOCRATES

Wing commanded by Alexander

MACEDONIAN CAVALRY LED BY ALEXANDER

Grancius River

Road to Zelea (through the Asiatic Gates)

AGRIANIAN INFANTRY

HYRCANIAN CAVALRY

LIGHT TROOPS OF MEMNON

LINE OF EXPLORERS

CILICIAN CAVALRY

PAPHLAGONIAN CAVALRY

BACTRIAN CAVALRY

MEDIAN CAVALRY

LINE OF GREEK MERCENARIES (HOPLITES)

Map of the battle with which, in May of 334 BC, Alexander won his first victory over the Persians. The two armies faced each other along the banks of the river. The Persians had the advantage of position, but Alexander overcame them with an astute and daring tactical maneuver. He threw himself into the thick of the hand-to-hand fighting, risking his life many times, and won a crushing victory over his enemy.

royal cavalry, led by Socrates, to cross the river and engage the Persians, while he outflanked the enemy position, making a hidden crossing of the Granicus with the valiant Agrianians and most of the cavalry. The plan succeeded, and while the cavalry of the satraps struggled to contain the attack led by Socrates and to counterattack in the direction of Parmenion, who had also crossed the river, Alexander unleashed the decisive charge against the strongest point in the Persian ranks.

In the furious battle that ensued, Alexander seriously risked losing his life. Attacked by the satraps, who had identified him, he used his lance to unhorse Mithridates but was surrounded by the enemy. With his lance broken and helmet hacked apart by a sword blow, he was about to be struck by Spithridates, who raised his scimitar to deliver the blow, when Cleitus, leading the royal squadron, broke through and sliced off the Persian's sword arm, thus saving Alexander's life. By then the

The battle of the Granicus in a painting by Charles Le Brun (1619–1690).

phalanxes of heavy infantry had managed to cross the river in formation and were engaging the enemy, using their sarissas to keep the Persian cavalry at bay. With their entire line broken, the cavalry of the satraps turned and fled. At that point Alexander ordered his men to attack the Greek mercenaries, who had remained in their position. It was a hard struggle and Alexander's horse was killed, but soon the mercenaries—to whom Alexander had determined to give no quarter—were massacred.

Alexander had won his first battle on Persian soil and, thanks to his tactics of surprise, had done so with minimal loses: only twenty-five Companions of the Macedonian cavalry and a few dozen infantry and cavalry from other units. The enemy dead on the field numbered in the thousands.

southward that led to Ionia, a region with numerous Greek cities from which Alexander could expect to receive help and supplies, lay open. Before moving his army, he entrusted Antigonus with the administration of the northern districts, naming him satrap of Phrygia. The country was beginning to have a new ruler.

In keeping with the propagandistic aspects of his expedition, Alexander sought to present himself to the Greek cities of Asia Minor as a liberator. Wherever they went, the Macedonian troops installed democratic governments endowed with self-determination. Doing so was very much to the advantage of the conqueror, since the Persians, not

Right: *Alexander and Craterus Fighting a Lion*, polychrome mosaic that decorated a wall in a house at Pella; Museum of Pella.

Above: Ruins of the ancient port of Miletus, now partially covered by seawater.

Opposite top: The Artemis of Ephesus; Museo Archeologico, Naples.

unlike Philip in Greece, had depended for their rule on tyrants and oligarchies. In this way Alexander succeeded in obtaining solid assistance from most of the towns on the coast. He did not apply his diplomatic talents only to Greeks. He also recognized the rights of the other subject populations in the Persian Empire, in particular the Lydians of Sardis, the capital of the satrapy. He took control of the city and its great wealth without a fight.

The battle of the Grancius delivered a powerful blow to Persian prestige and power. Throughout Asia Minor, all hope of putting a halt to the Greek advance was lost. The Great King realized that the situation was so grave that it required his personal intervention. Time was needed to assemble an army capable of driving out the invaders, since the troops had to arrive from even the most distant provinces. Meanwhile Memnon, the only general among the Persians to have demonstrated undeniable abilities, was sent to save what he could. He still had several major strongholds, including the important cities of Miletus and Halicarnassus, and most of all he could count on a fleet strong enough to pose a serious threat to the Greeks.

Alexander put all his trust in his troops on land, looking on his fleet as more of a

where he continued to threaten the Greek army. A kind of stalemate took hold, at least until Alexander managed to take control of all the ports in Asia Minor.

Meanwhile winter arrived, and the Greek soldiers were suffering exhaustion. Alexander sent Parmenion with a large part of the troops to spend the winter in Phrygia and granted home leave to all those Macedonian soldiers that had recently married. He then took a small force on a winter campaign in the southern provinces of the Anatolian peninsula, providing support to all the local potentates that opposed the Persians. In Caria, he restored to the throne Queen Ada, sister of both Pixodarus and also of the famous Mausolus, the ruler whose magnificent tomb, among the wonders of antiquity, is remembered in the word *mausoleum*. Queen Ada, who had no heirs, repaid Alexander by adopting him and naming him her successor.

During these months, at times using force but most often by way of diplomacy, Alexander was taking over control of the Persian administration. He collected tribute as the Great King in the regions

vexation than a help. The loyalty of the sailors seemed questionable, but more aggravating was the enormous cost of the ships, which drew heavily on his depleted treasury. Thus, although aware he risked losing control of the lines of communication with his homeland, he decided to dissolve the allied Greek fleet and to carry on the sieges of the enemy strongholds with only his army. The first to go was Miletus, which he took by land; he then concentrated his troops on Halicarnassus, which fell after a spirited resistance in the fall of 334 BC. The skilled Memnon, however, moved the bulk of his soldiers and his fleet to the island of Cos, from

Above: Metope with high-relief carving of a battle scene, dating to 200 BC; Museo Archeologico Nazionale, Taranto. This is an example of the funerary art of the area of Taranto, once part of Magna Graecia.

Right: *Alexander Cutting the Gordian Knot*, drawing by Vittorio Maria Bigari; Istituto di Storia dell'Arte, Fondazione Cini, Venice.

Opposite top: Persian guard armed with lance and shield in a fragment of a bas-relief that decorated the stairway of the Apadana Palace at Persepolis.

Opposite bottom: "The Persians," Apulian red-figure volute krater attributed to the Darius Painter and made in Canosa.

he ruled and replaced indigenous satraps with Macedonian officials. As word of his victories spread, the first legendary tales came into being, many of them invented and spread by the cunning Callisthenes. One early tale that enjoyed great fortune was the story of the Gordian knot.

This highly complicated knot of cords joining the shaft and yoke of an ancient chariot was preserved in a sanctuary. According to an ancient prophecy, whoever succeeded in untying the knot would become king of all Asia. Many had tried and all had failed. After failing in turn to untie the knot, Alexander drew his sword and cut the Gordian knot in half, handily solving the age-old problem in this unconventional way. Later he would prove the veracity of the prophecy.

Early that spring Memnon returned to the offensive, occupying islands in the Aegean Sea and blocking the naval routes between Asia and Europe.

These Persian initiatives offered hope to those Greeks hoping for independence from Macedonian rule, chief among them Sparta, to which the Persian king was providing financial support. Just when the situation seemed on the verge of becoming truly complicated, Alexander received word that Memnon, his most fearsome adversary, had fallen ill and died.

THE MARCH AGAINST THE GREAT KING

With the death of Memnon, command of the Persian army went directly into the hands of Darius III, who found himself forced to demonstrate his right to rule by confronting and driving out the Greek invaders. To this end he assembled an enormous army at Babylon, composed in large part of Persian troops and troops from the eastern satrapies. The core of the army was the palace guard of the Immortals, so called because their number was never fewer than 10,000. There were then the Royal Relations (a group of high officials more or less legitimately related to the king) and the Spear Bearers, who cleared the way for the king's chariot. This chariot was made of gleaming

gold, its yoke crusted with precious stones. Darius himself, tall and bearded, dressed in a white tunic and wearing his crown, rode on this chariot through the crowds of his faithful. Darius had made certain that his army, aside from its famous archers and fearsome iron-armored cavalry, had units of heavy infantry to take on the well-trained Macedonian phalanx. He had therefore enrolled another 30,000 Greek mercenaries and had created brigades of Cardace infantry, younger soldiers armed in the Macedonian manner. In total, the Great King's army was two or three times larger than Alexander's, although an enormous baggage train and the crowds of royal followers seriously compromised its mobility. As was Persian custom, Darius III traveled with hundreds of mules and camels that carried his family and his entire harem, composed of more than three hundred concubines. There were then hundreds of eunuchs and servants, aside from luxurious tents and costly plate and furnishings.

As soon as word of Darius's preparations reached him, Alexander assembled his army from all the various provinces and marched southward to find the Persians. In July of 333 BC, he crossed the fearsome Cilician Gates, where a small group of determined soldiers could have kept him blocked for months, encountering almost no real resistance and descending onto the sunny plains around Tarsus. Here, hot and covered in dust, Alexander took a swim in the cold waters of the Cydnus River; within a few hours he fell seriously ill, apparently on the point of death. Only the doctor called Philip the Greek, who had known Alexander since childhood, dared propose a cure. Although warned to stay away from the doctor—Parmenion claimed he had been bribed to kill him by the Great King—Alexander took the medicine Philip prepared and overcame the crisis, although his recovery took several weeks. When he regained his health, Alexander resumed the long march along the coast of today's Gulf of Iskenderun. Meanwhile, Darius

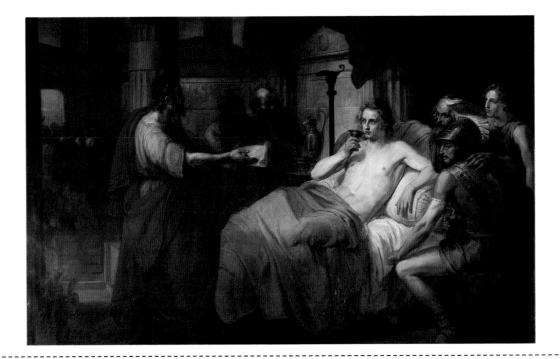

Right: *The Battle of Issus,* painting by Albrecht Altdorfer, 1529; Alte Pinakothek, Munich.

Opposite: *Alexander Drains the Cup of Medicine,* painting by Domenico Induno, 1836; Brera, Milan.

was slowly moving toward him. The two commanders moved ahead, neither aware of the other's whereabouts, and at a certain point the two armies passed each other without either spotting the other. So it was that at the end of October the Persian army suddenly found itself in the rear of the Greeks. When Darius realized this, he ordered his men to take up positions on the plain of Issus, on the banks of the Pinarus River. The site was not ideal for his troops, for the narrow plain, only about three miles wide, was poorly suited to the full deployment of the large Persian force. Alexander, as impetuous as ever, accepted battle despite his obvious numerical inferiority and had his men wheel about and form a line facing the enemy. The encounter was harsh and

brutal. The Persians seemed to have the upper hand in the beginning, but in the end Alexander won a complete victory, routing the Persian forces. But Alexander did not succeed in his primary objective, which was capturing Darius. Although he personally charged the Great King's war chariot, he failed to catch his enemy. Thanks to the sacrifice of his elite troops, who let themselves be massacred to permit him to escape, Darius managed to flee the battlefield. Even so, the Persian camp, along with the baggage train, royal treasury, and Darius's entire family, including his mother and wife, fell into Alexander's hands. The unthinkable had occurred: the ruler of Asia had been defeated on the field of battle and forced to flee. The symbols of his power, the royal mantle, bow, and chariot,

The Battle of Issus

At Issus, as at the Grancius, the Persian army took up a defensive position along the banks of a river, in this case the Pinarus. This time the Persian army was enormous and was commanded by the Great King himself. At the center of the formation Darius placed the Greek mercenaries and the Cardace infantry, with the bulk of the cavalry on the right flank, near the sea. Other troops occupied the heights, threatening the Greek right wing. When the Macedonian advance guard appeared on the plain, Darius, standing in his chariot at the center of the troops, commanded the cavalry to advance. Alexander, who arrived from the south, had his men halt so he could rapidly study the enemy position. He then deployed his army along a vast front that ran from the hills to the seacoast. Parmenion, as usual in command of the left wing, was now given the difficult task of halting the attack of the Persian cavalry. Meanwhile Alexander, with the Agrianians and the cavalry, attacked the Persian right wing, driving the enemy troops from

their positions on the heights and attacking in the direction of the left wing of the Persian formation. The cavalry of both sides battled furiously in the middle of the water and mud of the river while the infantry went into action in the center. Although arranged along an overly long front, the

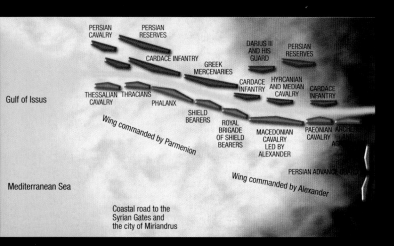

Left: Map of the battle of Issus, fought in November 333 BC. Amid the swirling battle, Alexander and Darius suddenly found themselves face to face.

Above: The Alexander Mosaic from Pompeii, which probably depicts the moment in which the two commanders saw each other.

Macedonian phalanx easily pushed through the Cardace infantry, but when it came up against the Greek mercenaries it ran the risk of being surrounded. Just as its wall of sarissas was coming apart, Alexander arrived on the scene, driving his cavalry through the hoplites and aiming at the chariot of the Great King. On the opposite wing, Parmenion had pushed aside the Persian heavy cavalry and the valiant Thessalian horsemen were closing the circle. Although the fighting continued to rage, Alexander's cavalry had the center of the Persian formation in pincers, and by the time darkness began to fall across the field of battle the outcome had been decided. Realizing the great danger he was in, Darius wheeled his chariot around and fled, leaving his brother Oxyathres, commander of the royal guard, to block the pursuit. For one moment Darius and Alexander,

who had made his way through the swirling mass, found themselves face to face. According to some, the two even exchanged lance blows, and the Great King may even have slightly wounded Alexander's thigh, but in the end Oxyathres, sacrificing most of his men, managed to cut off the pursuers and Darius was able to flee toward the hills. When the ground became too difficult for the chariot, the Persian ruler continued his flight on horseback, abandoning the chariot and with it the emblems of his power, later found by Macedonian troops. By then, night had fallen and Alexander, who had immediately set off after his adversary, had to suspend the operations. The Great King's escape was the only negative aspect of a spectacular victory, and Alexander found himself suddenly holding most of the Persian king's possessions.

had been taken by the Greeks, and Darius's family was held hostage by the victor.

Macedonian soldiers found the royal family wandering the camp in tears, mourning the death of the Great King. Alexander treated them with his usual chivalrous generosity. He went to them personally and assured them of the fate of Darius, giving orders that they were to be treated in accordance with their rank, most of all Sisygambis, Darius's mother, whom the Macedonian honored even more than the others, treating her almost as his own mother.

Plutarch

"After the battle Alexander went to wash himself in Darius's bath. . . . When he beheld the bathing vessels, the water-pots, the pans, and the ointment boxes, all of gold curiously wrought, and smelt the fragrant odors . . . he turned to those about him and said, 'This, it seems, is royalty.'"

A few weeks later, to crown the success, news reached Alexander that Antigonus, his lieutenant in Asia Minor, had defeated and annihilated the Persian troops that had fled the battlefield and tried to reorganize in the rear. In that inglorious way ended the last hopes tied to the army in which Darius had placed so much trust.

THE CONQUEST OF THE COASTS

It was not long before the results of the battle of Issus made themselves felt. The rich territories of Syria and the powerful cities of Phoenicia, such as Aradus, Byblos, and Sidon, passed to Alexander. Thus the last bases of operation of the Persian fleet fell without a blow. There was one notable exception. Tyre, the most important city in the region, was willing to formally accept the new ruler's authority but would not permit him to enter the city. Alexander, who had expressed the wish to offer sacrifice in the city's temple of Melkarth,

Right: The Alexander Sarcophagus from the royal necropolis of Sidon, ca. 320–310 BC; Archaeological Museum, Istanbul. The sarcophagus held the remains of Abdalonymus, made king of Sidon by Alexander.

Below: Bas-relief of a Phoenician warship.

Opposite: *Alexander and the Family of Darius* by Gaspare Diziani (1689–1767); Ca' Spineda, Treviso.

a Tyrian god identified by the Greeks with his ancestor Heracles, took the refusal as a serious provocation and gave orders to take the city by force. The inhabitants of Tyre felt safe. Standing on a well-fortified island separated from the coast by a wide stretch of sea and protected by a strong fleet, the city was considered impregnable. No army, not even that of the great king of Babylon, Nebuchadnezzar, who had laid siege to the city for thirteen years, had succeeded in taking it. In fact, the siege of Tyre proved difficult, the hardest of those undertaken by Alexander's army. The Tyrians, bolstered in part by the expectation (which was later proven to be groundless) that Carthaginian allies were coming to their aid, defended themselves with fanatical courage. Alexander's engineers made use of all their skills. They even constructed a mole connecting the city to the mainland, across which towers and other siege engines could be brought within reach of the city's walls. Meanwhile, the ships of the other Phoenician cities, by then allies of the Greeks, blocked the city's two ports. The Tyrians responded with tenacity and creativity. They sent underwater divers to cut the anchor cables of the Greek ships, used fire ships to destroy the siege towers on the mole, and fitted tridents and fishing nets to the walls to impale or trap the assailants. After eight months of battle, the simultaneous action of the fleet and the siege engines won out over the

resistance. Enraged by the atrocities committed by the Tyrians, who had even killed the heralds that came to ask their surrender, the Greek victors were ferocious. A large number of the inhabitants were killed, and more than 30,000 were sold into slavery. As he had done at Thebes, Alexander wanted to make clear the fate of those who dared resist him. He had 2,000 of the Tyrians crucified along the shore. In the middle of the smoking ruins of the sacked and destroyed city, Alexander

Siege Weapons

In the siege of Tyre and on other occasions, engineers and specialists in the construction and operation of siege machines supported Alexander's cavalry and infantry. Taking a fortified city was a complex affair, requiring the combined action of men and machines under the direction of expert engineers. The Macedonians could count on balistae and catapults powered by torsion springs that could strike targets up to 500 yards away. These weapons were transported disassembled as part of the army's baggage train. Defeating an enemy

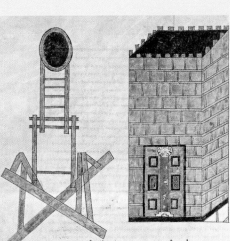

Siege machines in a miniature by Apollodoros of Damascus in the Codex Parisinus; Biblioteca Apostolica Vaticana, Rome.

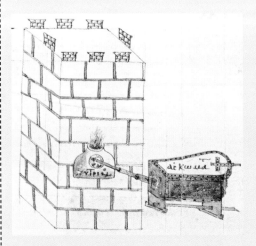

stronghold sometimes required the use of more specialized machines, and these would be built on the site. Alexander's chief engineer, a Thessalian named Diades, was able to construct "self-propelled," fire-resistant towers up to 200 feet high and large enough to hold not only archers and catapults but also drawbridges and iron-headed rams to bore into walls. At Tyre such structures were mounted on platforms attached to the decks of two side-by-side warships; in that way the ram could be brought to bear on any section of the city's walls. In all probability, it was these "ram-ships" that finally opened the decisive breach through which the assault troops first entered the city.

was finally able to make his sacrifice to the god. Having succeeded in protecting his lines of communication, and with nothing threatening his rear, he was now free to continue the war against the Persians.

During the course of the siege, Darius III had sought to initiate negotiations with the Greeks. These overtures came in the form of an exchange of letters and diplomats. In his first letter, Darius, worried about his family, declared himself ready to pay a large ransom for their freedom and offered Alexander friendship and an alliance, even the possession of vast territories of Asia Minor. Alexander responded proudly: he told the Great

Above: Oarsmen on a trireme, the light warship used by the Greeks, in a bas-relief from the fifth century BC; Museum of the Acropolis, Athens. The trireme had an agile hull, stabilized by blocks of stone as ballast, and three rows of oarsmen. The troops stood on the upper deck.

Below: Alexander and the family of Darius in a fresco by Pellegrino Tibaldi.

Arrian

"Your ancestors invaded Macedonia and the rest of Greece and did us great harm, though we had done them no prior injury; I have been appointed leader of the Greeks, and invaded Asia in the desire to take vengeance on Persia for your aggressions. . . . Although I marched against you, it was you that started the quarrel."

seized the Persian throne illegally, and that he was unworthy of ruling. "If you dispute your right to the kingdom," Alexander concluded brutally, "stand your ground and fight for it; do not run away, for I will come after you, wherever you go."

Despite the tone of this letter, Darius III did not lose hope of reaching an accord and sent a second letter in which he made even more appealing offers, including the hand of his daughter and all the territories up to the Euphrates. Many of Alexander's generals, including Parmenion, urged him to accept, but Alexander again refused, firmly convinced that he would achieve far more. In fact, his most recent victories had persuaded him that there were no serious impediments to his conquest of the entire Persian Empire. Just as this new rejection from Alexander arrived, Darius learned of the death of his beloved wife Stateira. The woman, who in keeping with Persian tradition was wife and sister of the Great

King that from now on he should address him as a superior and claimed that he had come to seek revenge for all the injustices the Greeks had suffered at the hands of the Persians, including the invasions of Darius and Xerxes and the assassination of Philip, which Alexander now claimed had been ordered by the Persian king. He also stated that Darius was only a usurper, having

Opposite top: Darius dictates a message for Alexander, miniature from the *Khamse* by Nezami, fifteenth-century Indian manuscript.

Opposite bottom: *The Death of the Wife of Darius,* by Louis Lagrenée (1725–1805); Louvre, Paris.

King, had died in childbirth in the Macedonian camp, and Alexander arranged a royal funeral ceremony for her. Saddened by the two items of bleak news, Darius decided to risk everything by organizing an unbeatable army. To do so meant assembling troops from every part of his immense empire, from the Persian Gulf to India, a difficult undertaking that would require at least a year.

Alexander, who for the moment was following his plan to take control of all the costal regions, was still collecting the fruits of his victories. Parmenion, his right arm, occupied Damascus, taking hold of immense spoils, enough to free Alexander from any immediate financial worries. Finally, even Alexander, until then indifferent to feminine graces, permitted himself distraction in the arms of a woman. The chosen was the beautiful and learned Barsine, widow of Memnon and daughter of a satrap who had been the guest in Macedonia of Philip II. It was probably Barsine, at the time thirty years old and fluent in both Greek and Persian, who got Alexander to refine his cultural studies. A few years later Barsine gave

Above: Alexander receives a letter from Darius and symbolic gifts: a whip, ball, and gold box; Istituto Ellenico di Studi Bizantini e Post-Bizantini, Venice.

Below: Bronze portrait bust of the young Alexander with foliate gilding, second century BC; Museo Nazionale Romano.

birth to a son, whom Alexander named Heracles in honor of the mythical founder of his dynasty.

Not even the graces of Barsine could long distract the conqueror, and soon he resumed his march southward along the sea toward Egypt, along the way accepting the surrender of various minor cities. Things were different at Gaza, where the Greeks came up against stubborn resistance.

The city, under its governor Batis, a eunuch faithful to Darius III, dominated the plain from above a hill and was defended by a seasoned garrison of Arabian mercenaries. Once again Alexander's engineers had to use their ingenuity. They constructed a high mound on which to operate siege towers and catapults to strike the enemy from above, while sappers dug tunnels and shafts beneath the city's walls. In this way, the Greeks managed to create breaks in the wall through which they entered the city. As always, Alexander was among the first in, and he received two wounds. This did not prevent him from taking the city and ordering a new massacre. All the men were killed and the women and children sold into slavery. Alexander gave Batis the same treatment Achilles gave Hector: he was tied by the ankles to the back of a chariot and dragged in the dirt around the walls. With this new proof of ferocity, suggested by his reading of Homer, the Macedonian opened the way to Egypt.

EGYPT

The rich land of the Nile, still permeated with its ancient culture, had never been completely bent to Persian domination. Since the period of its original conquest two centuries earlier, at the time of Cambyses, there had been continuous revolts in Egypt against foreign rule, most of all in the region of the delta, the most difficult to control. Over the last seventy years, the country had won back its independence under various pharaohs. The last of these indigenous rulers, Nectanebo II, had been defeated and put to flight by Artaxerxes III only ten years earlier. A period had followed of somewhat harsh Persian domination. Unlike his predecessors, who had always respected the religion of the country, Artaxerxes III had shown little tolerance for his rebellious subjects and had made himself odious with sacrilegious acts and damages done to priests and temples alike. He was said to have shown his contempt for local customs by having the sacred bull of the god Apis killed and roasted and had even eaten it, an act that outraged the local

people. Alexander knew he could profit from this unstable situation by drawing on the resentment the Egyptians harbored for their Persian rulers.

In little more than a week's time, Alexander crossed the inhospitable region between Gaza and Egypt, and he entered that country almost unopposed. The last Persian satrap, whose

Opposite: The Pharaoh Nectanebo II between the feet of the god Horus in a sculpture reminiscent of one presenting the pharaoh Khafre protected by the falcon-god Horus, but with the proportions inverted, making the divinity far larger than the king.

Above: Head of Nectanebo I, successor to Nepherites II and first pharaoh of Egypt's thirtieth dynasty.

Right: Alexander and the statue of Nectanebo in a miniature of *The Romance of Alexander* (manuscript by the scribe Nersès).

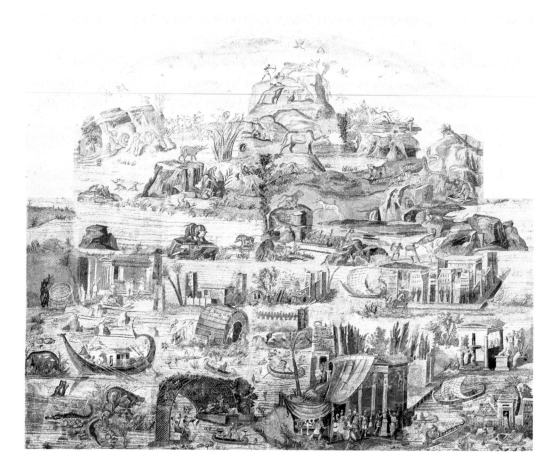

forces had been recently worn out by a revolt of Greek mercenaries led by a renegade Macedonian, peacefully ceded the province, putting himself at Alexander's disposal. At that point Alexander, astutely behaving in a manner opposite to that of Artaxerxes, paid open tribute to the gods of the Egyptians, following the rites of the ancient pharaohs. At Memphis he sacrificed to the sacred bull Apis, and at Karnak and Luxor ordered the restoration of the sanctuaries profaned by the Persians. In this way, he assured himself of the benevolence of the local populace, and most of all the support of the priests of the great temples, the true power in the country. They accepted him as their new sovereign, crowning him pharaoh and saluting him as the divine son of the sun god

Amun-Ra. Alexander, for his part, assumed the task of defending the country and his new subjects and guaranteeing the continuation of administrative functions and religious practices. He entrusted the religious practices to two Egyptians, delegated to represent the monarch in Upper and Lower Egypt, while defense and financial matters were entrusted to Greek and Macedonian officials.

Without doubt, the evocative nature of ancient Egyptian civilization deeply affected Alexander, but he never forgot that he was a Greek and that his duty was to spread Greek culture to all the newly conquered lands. For example, wherever he went he organized sporting events, theatrical presentations, and literary competitions in keeping with the customs of his homeland. In the same way he supported and protected the Greek trading centers established along the delta. His most important and enduring act in Egypt was the foundation of a new city at the mouth of the

Above: The Lighthouse of Alexandria in a reconstruction by H. Thiersch.

Right: Model of the lighthouse; Musée Maritime, Alexandria.

Opposite top: Mosaic showing scenes of daily life on the banks of the Nile; Museo Prenestino-Barberiniano, Palestrina (Rome).

Opposite bottom: Limestone head of Alexander wearing the pharaonic uraeus, third century BC; Museo Archeologico, Naples.

Alexander's Dream

Like that of many other famous cities of antiquity, legend surrounds the foundation of Alexandria. Plutarch reports that Alexander chose the site after being inspired by certain lines in the Odyssey, which he had heard in a dream spoken by Homer himself: "An island lies, where loud the billows roar/Pharos they call it, on the Egyptian shore." Always responsive to inspiration from the beloved poet, Alexander immediately ordered his architects to trace out the perimeter of the new city, its shape roughly based on that of a Macedonian cloak. Since chalk was not available, the lines were traced on the ground with barley flour. Alexander was pleased with the result, but so were the local birds, which swooped upon the flour in flocks and devoured every morsel in no time at all. Almost all those present interpreted this as a bad omen, but Alexander's soothsayer, Aristander, was on hand and, as usual, found a way to interpret the omen in a light that served Alexander's needs, declaring that it meant the future city would be so prosperous as to nourish the peoples of many nations. His prophecy was destined to prove true, for Alexandria became the commercial center to which the rich harvests of Egyptian agriculture were brought for distribution throughout the Mediterranean world.

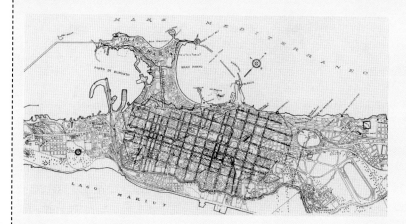

Above: "Pompey's Pillar," the granite column built during the reign of Diocletian on the hill of the Serapeum.

Left: Map comparing ancient and modern Alexandria.

western branch of the Nile, opposite the island of Pharos. With happy intuition he chose as the site for the city a sandy tongue of land separating an interior lagoon from the sea, making it a kind of symbolic link between Egypt and the rest of the world. This locality had numerous advantages: it was easy to defend and had water resources, a temperate climate, and good anchorage. The construction was planned with great care, following

Tomb and courtyard from the Hellenistic period in the necropolis of Mustafa Pasha. Such funerary monuments are among the few remaining traces of the Hellenistic period of Alexandria.

the precepts of Greek city-building. The intent, however, was not only to create a city in which Greeks could live according to their traditions but also to create a place where diverse ethnic communities could live together peacefully and prosper. Alexander named this new city—destined to soon become one of the most important metropolises of antiquity—after himself, beginning a custom he was to maintain throughout his life.

With the foundation of the city of Alexandria, Alexander gave expression to the most rational aspects of his complex character. There were also dark and inscrutable sides to his personality, as was revealed by the expedition he undertook to the oasis of Siwah. This oasis was the site of an ancient oracular divinity of Libyan origin, the ram-headed god Ammon, once identified by the Egyptians with the sun god Amun-Ra and by the Greeks with Zeus. Animated by a desire that moderns can find difficult to understand, Alexander, accompanied by a small contingent, traveled to the west along the cost and then, confronting dangers and discomforts, turned to head inland across nearly three hundred miles of desert. When he reached the remote sanctuary, Alexander asked to confer alone with the priests. What he asked and what the priests answered have remained secret, but contemporaries hypothesized that Alexander had asked the god to reveal the secret of his birth. In all probability the oracle told the young conqueror what he wanted to hear, that he was not the son of Philip but rather of Zeus-Ammon. From then on, Alexander took to boasting of his divine descent, at first only when among close friends but then more and more openly with others. This descent from Ammon, which naturally excluded Philip, displeased many of the Macedonian veterans who had served under the former ruler, but it was greeted with favor by many Greeks, most of all those originally from Asia Minor, more ready to accept miraculous revelations. After all, the greatest heroes of Hellas, such as Hercules and Theseus, had been born to mixed divine and human parents, and on the cultural plane the idea did not present an insurmountable

Left: Bust of Zeus-Ammon, second century BC, discovered in the eighteenth century in the lower Rhone valley near the ruins of an ancient chapel. The ram horns were a characteristic of the divinity.

Opposite top: Alexander performing an offering to Amun-Ra, detail of a relief from the Temple of Luxor.

Opposite bottom: Stele with inscription about Samtowetefnakhte, found at Pompeii; Museo Archeologico, Naples.

up, and he was joined there by reinforcements sent by Antipater. With his ranks strengthened by these precious new troops, Alexander set off toward Asia.

The time had come to once again seek out Darius, and this time to deliver the final blow.

problem. The miraculous conception of Olympias and the mythical birth of Alexander were soon to become effective weapons of propaganda.

While in Egypt, Alexander received news that the final pieces of the Persian fleet had been broken

Plutarch

"Alexander asked the priest whether any of his father's murderers had escaped punishment, and the priest charged him to speak with more respect, since his was not a mortal father. Then Alexander desired to know if any of those who murdered Philip had been punished, and further, concerning dominion, whether the empire of the world was reserved for him. The god answered positively to both questions."

The Conquest of an Empire

*Having conquered the coasts, Alexander delivered the
final blow to the Persian Empire, destroying it forever.
But even the death of the Great King, chased into the
heart of Asia, did not bring an end to the war.*

THE LAST BATTLE WITH DARIUS III

In April of 331 BC, Alexander left Egypt and headed north, through Palestine and Phoenicia. At Samaria, where rebels had burned alive the Macedonian governor, he ordered a ferocious revenge that nearly depopulated the region, preparing it for future colonization. Along the way Alexander also oversaw the organization of the conquered territories, which were divided in two large administrative districts that included all the old satrapies. During this same period, he began

drawing on the treasure accumulated during his conquests to mint coins with his effigy. These coins soon spread as the means of payment throughout the region, first alongside and then replacing the old Persian darics.

Darius had not been inactive during Alexander's Egyptian campaign. The Great King had had time to assemble in Babylon the military forces from Persia and from the Upper Satrapies, the empire's far-eastern provinces. In answer to his call, the valiant horsemen of Bactria and Sogdiana, Media, Anatolia, and even India arrived in Babylon, as did groups of nomadic Scythians. Contingents of soldiers faithful to the Persian king were assembled even in Cappadocia and other regions that had fallen to Greek control. To make this force even more powerful, Darius decided to make use of special weapons, most of all

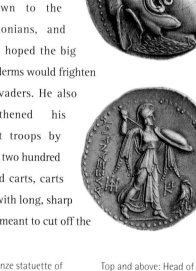

elephants, fifteen of which he planned to put in his front line. These animals were unknown to the Macedonians, and Darius hoped the big pachyderms would frighten the invaders. He also strengthened his assault troops by adding two hundred scythed carts, carts fitted with long, sharp blades meant to cut off the

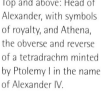

Left: Bronze statuette of Alexander from the first century AD; the work recalls a famous sculpture by Lysippos; Museo Archeological, Parma.

Top and above: Head of Alexander, with symbols of royalty, and Athena, the obverse and reverse of a tetradrachm minted by Ptolemy I in the name of Alexander IV.

limbs of infantrymen. Only his infantry, with the exception of the usual trusted Greek mercenaries, was decidedly inferior to that of Alexander. After the poor showing of the Cardace infantry at Issus, Darius decided this time to emphasize his other resources. It is thought that the total forces assembled by the Persian ruler numbered between 100,000 and 250,000 men. Darius III thus commanded three or four times as many soldiers than did Alexander.

Unaware of the preparations being made by his enemies, Alexander continued his advance, now moving to the east. Around the middle of July, he sent Hephaistion ahead to throw a bridge across the Euphrates. Having foreseen this move, the Persians sent the satrap Mazaeus to the opposite bank of the river. A general with a glorious past, he had been instructed to carry out a scorched-earth campaign and to keep the invaders from crossing the river. But on the arrival of the bulk of the Greek troops, Mazaeus abandoned his position. Alexander had a bridge built of rafts lashed together with iron chains, got his

Above: Ahura-Mazda, god of the Achaemenids and protector of the Persian rulers, presented in a winged disk in a relief at Persepolis.

Below: Intaglio of first century AD showing Alexander as Achilles, his mythical ancestor on his maternal line; Museo Archeologico, Naples.

army across, and headed into Assyria, where the mountains made for a bearable climate even during the summer. He moved at a forced march toward the Tigris just as Darius, too, was moving toward the eastern bank of the river.

By then, both contenders were seeking a major confrontation. For Darius it meant the chance to win much-desired revenge; for Alexander it meant the final act in his conquest of the Persian Empire. Alexander reached the Tigris River, fully expecting to find the Persians waiting for him. Instead, he found no one. His army was thus able to make the crossing undisturbed, making camp on the opposite shore. Losing an excellent opportunity to catch the enemy at a moment of inferiority, Darius had chosen another field for the battle, the vast plain of Gaugamela, not far from the ruins of Nineveh, the ancient capital of the Assyrians, by then little more than a group of uninhabited ruins.

Hoping to avoid the error committed at Issus, this time Darius chose the site for the battle with great care. He even had his men level the plain to facilitate the movement of the carts and had snares and stakes spread across the areas where he expected the Greek cavalry to charge.

At the end of September, encouraged by an event seen as a good omen—an eclipse that the alert soothsayer Aristander interpreted as the sunset of the Persian Empire—the Greek troops marched boldly toward Darius's army. The night of the twenty-ninth, however, the soldiers were faced with the discouraging sight of the thousands of campfires lit by their enemy. In front of them spread an enormous army, the largest they had ever seen. They were gripped by panic. Alexander did his best to calm his soldiers, but even he was uneasy and spent the night with Aristander, making sacrifices to ensure the favor of the gods. For the first and only time, Alexander killed a victim in honor of Phobus, god of the fear that disturbs minds. The next morning, having regained his legendary courage, Alexander rode around the field of battle with a few companions to study the defenses put in place by Darius and to finalize the plan of attack. On the morning of October 1, after sleeping serenely, he put on his damascened armor and plumed helmet, mounted his faithful Bucephalus, and addressed his soldiers, making an appeal to Zeus, the divine father.

As could easily have been foreseen, the encounter was ferocious, with the outcome uncertain for most of the day. Under the command of Mazaeus and Bessus, a relative of Darius, the wings of the Persian army attempted to encircle the Greeks. But once again, Alexander and a group of select warriors punched a hole in the Persian ranks and attacked toward the center, precisely where Darius was.

As at Issus, the Great King—who enjoyed fame for great personal courage—abandoned his position and fled while the outcome of the battle was still undecided. He probably hoped to organize a final

Right: Painting by Gustave Moreau (1826–1898) showing Darius drinking from a well while in flight from the battle.

Opposite top: Bronze model of a Macedonian helmet, fourth century BC. This is the Phrygian or Thracian type, which appeared in Greece in the fifth century BC and spread to the Italic and Etruscan areas.

Opposite bottom: Darius III on his war chariot flees the battle of Gaugamela on an amphora from ca. 330–320 BC by the so-called Darius Painter. The complex mythological and historic scene is arranged on two levels divided by a decorative band.

The Battle of Gaugamela

After his experience at Issus, Darius III, aware that the next battle would prove decisive, made sure his army would be completely superior to that of the Greeks at Gaugamela. Following the plan prepared for the empire's traditional forces, the Great King, surrounded by his immense army, overwhelmed the Persian horsemen that Bessus and Mazaeus, Darius's lieutenants, sent to encircle the Greeks. The scythed carts also failed to achieve good results. Agrianian javelins soon knocked the drivers from their positions. Having driven back these attacks, Alexander immediately charged with his cavalry against the bulk of the Persian army, having spotted its weak point. Raising their war cry of *Aalalalalai*, Alexander's warriors charged into the center of the Persian ranks, throwing it into total confusion. A few thousand determined

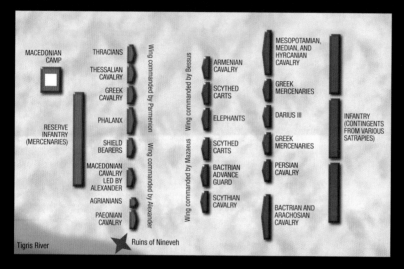

faithfully awaited the beginning of the battle. But he had underrated the military genius of his adversary. Alexander presented what appeared to be his usual formation, but in reality he had added infantry units to the wings and a second row of infantry to the rear guard, transforming his army into a giant, unassailable block. A little before noon the two armies went into action. On the dry plain the hooves of the horses raised enormous clouds of dust that reduced visibility to a few yards. Alexander profited from this to move his assault troops to the right, a movement that was unseen by the Persians. These, backed by infantry,

Above: Map of the battle of Gaugamela. Here again Alexander displayed his military genius with astonishing results, succeeding in defeating the far more numerous troops of Darius III. Only the breakthrough in the Greek line caused by the elephants and the scythed carts, which required the attention of the Macedonian cavalry, prevented Alexander from achieving a perfect victory.

Right: *The Battle of Gaugamela*, by Jan Bruegel; Louvre, Paris.

soldiers broke the resistance of a far larger body of troops. When Alexander spotted Darius's chariot, he rushed toward it, hurling his lance. Things were going less well for the Macedonians at the center and on the left wing. The Shield Bearers and Foot Companions, remembering the lesson learned from the Triballians, managed to avoid being run over by the elephants and the scythed carts, but in doing so created a large opening into which streamed Persian and Indian troops eager to sack the Greek camp.

By then Alexander had overcome most of the soldiers around Darius, but he was now forced to pull several cavalry squadrons out of the front line and send them to help in the rear. Thus, while the battle raged on, Darius again turned his chariot and fled in the dust, making his escape down the royal road. Not even the flight of the Great King could diminish Alexander's final victory: even in the eyes of many of his enemies, the Macedonian king was seen as the new ruler of Asia.

resistance in the Upper Satrapies. Alexander, summoned by Parmenion, whose troops were facing serious difficulty, was unable to take up the pursuit, and again Darius escaped. Even so, the importance of what had occurred that day was not lost on those who were on the field: the victory at Issus had had its definitive confirmation, and the outcome of the war had been decided. On the field of battle, Alexander's soldiers proclaimed him the king of Asia. Once again grasping the value of propaganda, he sought to give the event a Panhellenic character, sending a message to the Greeks announcing that revenge had been taken and proclaiming the end of all tyrannies and liberty for all the cities of Hellas. As usual, he sent a portion of the spoils to Europe, including gifts to the Italian town of Crotone, the only one in Magna Graecia that participated in the war against Xerxes.

In the Heart of the Empire

The day after the battle, by which time all hope of catching Darius had been lost, Alexander gave orders to break camp and move toward Babylonia, where he hoped to procure new provisions. Alexander had not forgotten what he had learned from his famous naturalist teacher, and along the road he stopped to study the strange flammable liquids that rose from the ground in that region. This was the Greeks' first encounter with petroleum. They learned of its dangers when a young boy, by way of experiment, volunteered to be soaked in the liquid and set alight: he was horribly burned.

Babylon, the rich capital of Mesopotamia, was well fortified and would have been able to hold out against the Greeks for a long time. The battle that had just ended, however, had enormously impressed many imperial officials, convincing them that the Achaemenid rule was at an end. So it was, that when Alexander's soldiers cautiously approached the formidable bastions of Semiramis, instead of a closed portal and walls packed with defenders, they found an open gate and a festive welcoming committee. At its head was Mazaeus, the same powerful satrap of Babylonia and general that had commanded the

Right: Fragment of a Lesbos marble stele, from 330–329 BC, with the inscription of a decree, from Mytilene; Archaeological Museum, Mytilene.

Babylon

One of the world's most famous cities, Babylon was so ancient it was said to have always existed. The city rose on the banks of the Euphrates, about sixty miles from today's Baghdad, on a fertile plain crossed by a vast network of irrigation canals. According to tradition, it had been founded by Sargon, king of Akkad, but he had probably only enlarged a village that already had been flourishing at the time of the Sumerians, more than 4,500 years ago. Over its multimillennial history, it had been home to many famous rulers, among them Hammurabi and Nebuchadnezzar, and had been the capital of powerful states until 539 BC, when it was conquered by Cyrus the Great and incorporated into the Persian Empire as the capital of the satrapy of Mesopotamia. Although the Persians neglected the religious and cult buildings from the time of Xerxes on, when Alexander arrived in Babylon it was still one of the most precious jewels of the East, with its splendid monuments, giant walls with majestic gates, and luxurious hanging gardens. Its streets were full of an alluring mixture of Arabs, Armenians, Persians, Jews, and Indians, and fabulous parties with banquets, dancing, and games took place in the elegant homes of the wealthy, located in the city quarter along the banks of the river. In that true earthly paradise, the conquerors, helped by generous disbursements from the city treasures, were able to leave behind the three years of deprivations and suffering.

Above: *Alexander Enters Babylon,* engraving by Charles Le Brun.

Below: The Gate of Ishtar at Babylon; reconstruction in the Pergamum Museum, Berlin.

Right: The recto and verso of a clay tablet of 507 BC, perhaps from Persepolis; Yale Babylonian Collection, New Haven. The text is written in late Elamite, one of the languages of the Achaemenid Persian Empire.

Below: Limestone capital with bulls' heads, one of the thirty-six interior columns of the royal palace at Susa.

right wing of the Persian army at Gaugamela. Accompanied by three sons and religious and civic authorities, he now hastened to pay homage to the man he had only a few days earlier done his best to kill. Alexander repaid him by reconfirming his position, the only change being the addition of a Macedonian official and a Greek administrator. Riding a triumphal cart, Alexander then made his majestic entry into Babylon, its streets strewn with flowers and adorned with garlands. He was acclaimed by the crowd, which had erected silver altars and now covered him in gifts. The ceremonies ended in the handing over of the citadel and the royal treasury. In Babylon, as in Egypt, Alexander sought to behave in accordance with local traditions and won over the sympathies of the priests, who looked with favor on the end of two centuries of Persian domination. As in the other territories, Alexander styled himself a local ruler, offering sacrifices to the principal divinity of the city, Bel-Marduk, and ordering the reconstruction of the temples destroyed by Xerxes, including the great temple dedicated to the protector

of the city and the ziggurat of Etemenanki, the gigantic construction that is the origin of the myth of the Tower of Babel.

Alexander set an important precedent in his treatment of Mazaeus and the other Persian officials, most of all by reinstating them in their positions, for this had vast repercussions. In no time, the satraps in other capital cities of the empire began abandoning Darius. At Susa, capital of Elam and one of the most illustrious Achaemenid cities, the governor surrendered without a fight, handing over the enormous treasure amassed in the palaces of the rulers: more than fifteen hundred tons of gold in the form of raw metal and royal darics. As he had done in Babylon and the other conquered lands, Alexander instructed that a portion of these riches be used to mint coins. The sudden influx of this new capital, a good part of which reached Asia Minor and Greece, had a powerful impact on economies throughout the eastern Mediterranean. Alexander's advance into these distant, unknown territories was leaving traces and also having an effect on him. As he moved

Above: Detail of a decorative frieze from the royal palace of Darius I at Susa. Made in relief using painted and glazed bricks, it presents a lion-griffon with ram's horns; Louvre, Paris.

Right: Alexander presented in the pages of a medieval manuscript; Armenian Mechitarist Congregation, San Lazzaro, Venice.

farther and farther east, Alexander was more and more influenced by the customs and traditions of the subject peoples, and over time this changed his politics and his idea of sovereignty. With every new success, he identified himself more with the Eastern concept of royalty and responded with great seriousness and understanding to the expectations of his new subjects, who for their part treated him with all the respect reserved for the Great King. In adopting this new behavior, Alexander slowly broke with the military austerity that had been instilled in him as a child and to which he had so long remained faithful. The change showed up in a series of clearly symbolic gestures. At Susa, for example, Alexander, hoping to give clear proof of his role as successor to the Achaemenids, sat on the tall, golden throne of the Persian kings. (The more malicious commentators

Persepolis

Founded in 518 BC by Darius I on the banks of the Pulvar River, in today's central-southern Iran, Persepolis, the ceremonial capital of the Persian Empire, was designed to be symbolic of the earthly power of the Great King, an enduring emblem of the benevolence of Ahura-Mazda and the other gods. The celebrative aspects were particularly apparent in the royal palace, located on an artificial platform sixty feet high that was reached by way of a monumental stairway. The various buildings that composed the palace included two enormous assembly halls, a treasury room, royal apartments, and rooms for the guards and harem, all of them closed with bronze doors. The walls were of brick decorated with gold and enamel and stood more than sixty feet high; the roofs were supported by massive columns of wood and marble with capitals carved in the shapes of bulls or fantastic creatures. Every year emissaries from all the many peoples of the empire came to these elegant rooms to bring tributes to the Great King. He awaited them in a highly dramatic room with one hundred columns, seated on his gold throne, scepter in hand, assisted by a slave whose function was to swat away flies. This magnificent ceremony, which had been repeated for more than two hundred years, represented the culminating moment of Persian power, and even today one can get an idea of what it was like from the reliefs that decorate the stairways of Persepolis.

Left: The eastern side of the Gate of Xerxes at Persepolis (Iran). The city was founded in 518 BC by Darius I and became the empire's ceremonial capital.

pointed out that whereas the tall Persians had sat on the throne with their feet on a footstool, the shorter Alexander had to rest his feet on a table.)

Alexander sat on Darius's throne, but the time had not yet come to lay aside weapons. He still had to eliminate all possible pockets of resistance, denying his adversaries every hope of revenge. With this objective in mind, he marched toward Persia, the region of origin of the empire and cradle of the royal Achaemenid dynasty. This time the Greek troops met tenacious resistance. From positions near the Gates of Persia, the Persian highlanders struggled to block the conqueror's path, fighting courageously. Alexander put them to flight after taking them in the rear, but this resistance made him realize that not all the subjects of Darius were ready to throw down their arms. This unexpected reaction, together with the discovery that some Greek prisoners had been mutilated, so upset him that when, in January of 330 BC, he arrived in Persepolis, ceremonial capital of the empire, he had

his soldiers sack the city even though he had already accepted the surrender of its defenders. Given a free hand, the troops carried out a true slaughter, devastating one of the world's most opulent cities. Only the splendid royal place was spared, and not for long. A few months later, in May, during one of the habitual wine-soaked Macedonian banquets, amid revelry in which all the participants gave in to drunkenness and their baser instincts, someone— according to some sources it was an Athenian courtesan named Thais—called on the assembled host to set fire to the great hall of Xerxes as revenge for the destruction of Greek temples. The idea was accepted, and within a few hours the glorious residence of the Persian kings had been reduced to a pile of ashes. This act, in certain ways inexplicable, marked the last time that Alexander behaved as the avenger of the Greeks. Indeed, from then on, his behavior changed, eventually coming to assume completely the role of new ruler of the empire and successor to the Great King. Greece and

his interest was now Asia, the land of conquest, a boundless empire far more vast than his European possessions. This empire had to be consolidated, however, and pacified, which required soothing his new Persian subjects. So it was that in the heart of Achaemenid territory, aside from confirming the Persian satrap in his post, Alexander sought to behave in accordance with local customs, even going to Pasargadae to pay homage at the tomb of Cyrus the Great, founder of the great empire of his enemies.

THE PURSUIT

The war could not yet be considered over. The battle of Gaugamela had certainly marked the end of Darius's power, but so long as he was alive the legitimacy of the conquest would be in doubt. During those last months, Darius took refuge at Ecbatana (modern Hamadan), capital of the satrapy of Media and summer residence of the Persian kings. There, amid temples and magnificent palaces covered in gold and silver, he still dreamed of revenge while awaiting reinforcements that never arrived. In the spring Alexander marched toward the city, and on learning of his approach, Darius quickly abandoned it, withdrawing to the east, where he expected the support of the soldiers of Bactria and Sogdiana. Thus the last of the great royal Persian capitals fell into Alexander's hands. At that point Alexander decided that the war he had fought in the name of the League of Corinth had come to an end. He wanted it made known that from now on his undertaking assumed a different character with infinitely greater objectives than those deliberated by the Panhellenic assembly. He sent all the allied contingents home, keeping with him only those soldiers who agreed to fight for him in his personal adventure. He then set about preparations to pursue the Great King, using only

Macedonia became far-off places, and the events that took place there were of almost no concern to the great conqueror. For example, when word reached him that his lieutenant Antipater had put a final end to the insurrection of the Spartans, defeating them in a battle at Megalopolis where their leader, King Agis, had been killed, thus finally establishing complete Macedonian supremacy, Alexander had nothing to say except that this important success was only "a battle of mice, not men." The center of

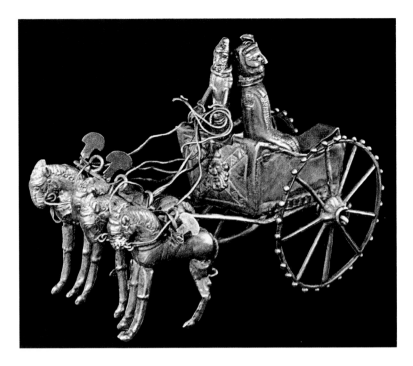

Right: Cart drawn by three horses from the treasure of Oxus, sixth to fifth century BC; British Museum, London.

Below: Thessalian horseman in a bas-relief found at Pelinna; Louvre, Paris.

Opposite: Hoplite with heavy armor, relief on the base of a statue from the fifth century BC; National Museum, Athens. With a plumed Corinthian helmet tipped back on his head, lance, shield, breastplate, and greaves, this infantryman is in keeping with the epic literary tradition.

his most mobile troops. At Ecbatana he left the ever-faithful Parmenion, charged with the task of overseeing the treasures of the city and protecting the communication route to the Mediterranean. In the belief that they would soon be reunited, the young king and the old general, who had played such an important role in the Macedonian victories, exchanged only a brief farewell. They were never to see each other again.

Darius may have hoped that Alexander would be satisfied with the endless territory he had conquered and would not continue the war; if he did so, he was seriously underestimating Alexander's tenacity and ambition. Alexander was moving ahead in a forced march, closely pursuing the few enemy troops he encountered. In eleven days, the Macedonians reached

Rhagae, near today's Teheran, where they learned that Darius had crossed the Caspian Gates and was seeking refuge in Hyrcania. This new headlong flight delivered the final blow to the Great King's prestige, even in the eyes of the few important aristocrats that had remained faithful to him. By then it was clear to all his subjects that Darius was unable to defend the empire and that the supreme god Ahura-Mazda was not going to accord him protection. At that point, the Persian nobles of the eastern provinces, lead by Bessus and the satraps Barsentes and Satibarzanes, decided to act. Darius, who had not wanted to put his trust in his faithful Greek mercenaries, was taken prisoner, and Bessus, who could boast of belonging to the Achaemenid line, proclaimed himself his successor with the name Artaxerses V. The deposed ruler, bound in golden chains,

Sometime later a Macedonian soldier in search of water found an abandoned wagon. In it was the mortally wounded Great King. Before fleeing, Satibarzanes and Barsentes had stabbed him, leaving Darius to die slowly in the desert. By the time Alexander reached the wagon, Darius had died. Clearly moved by the death of his adversary, Alexander performed a final noble act, removing his own cloak and wrapping it around the dead body.

THE NEW RULER OF ASIA

At the death of Darius, most of the Iranian nobles gathered around Alexander, who openly stated that he intended to treat the dead sovereign as the legitimate ruler and that Darius would be buried according to Persian rituals. The body of the Great King was entombed with all honors at Persepolis, where the other Achaemenids were buried, and his

was loaded on a wagon and taken toward Bactria. Learning of these events from stragglers, Alexander left Craterus in command of the bulk of the force and set off immediately with a few picked horsemen. Two days later they reached the camp where the treason had taken place. The pursuit continued at greater speed. Sixteen hours later Alexander and his exhausted men arrived at the village on the edge of the Dasht-i-Kavir desert where Bessus had spent the night. Learning from the inhabitants of a shortcut through the desert, but with no available water, Alexander mounted five hundred of his men on the surviving horses and continued the chase without stopping. After sixty miles, at the first light of dawn, they made out the enemy column and charged it. Bessus and his followers fled across the plain, leaving their baggage wagons to Alexander. The Macedonians searched the carts, but found no sign of Darius.

faithful followers were welcomed and protected by Alexander, who even enrolled Darius's brother, Oxyathres, in his personal guard. Since Alexander had once accused Darius of being only a usurper, this behavior marked a very striking change, and his soldiers witnessed it with growing perplexity. More surprises were yet to come. Most of the Macedonians, weary of a campaign that had dragged on for years, had joyfully welcomed the death of Darius, convinced

Above: Subject peoples bearing homage in a frieze of the Apadana Palace, Persepolis.

Opposite top: Head of a king in silver gilt from the Sassanid period in Iran, fourth century AD; Metropolitan Museum of Art, New York.

Opposite bottom: Dhu al-Qarnayn enthroned, from a manuscript of *Book of Animals* of Al-Jahiz compiled between the eighth and ninth century; Biblioteca Ambrosiana, Milan. In Islamic culture Alexander was identified with the "two-horned" king of the Koran's book of Revelation.

Arrian

"This was the end of Darius ... No man showed less spirit or sense in warfare, but in other matters he committed no offense, perhaps for the lack of opportunity, since the moment of his accession was also the moment of the attack on him by the Macedonians and Greeks."

it marked the end, that the time had finally come to return home and enjoy the wealth accumulated during the war. Alexander soon disabused them. To consolidate the empire he had conquered, he intended to capture and punish Bessus and the other satraps who had betrayed the man he now looked upon as his predecessor on the throne. Before the astonished and increasingly suspicious eyes of the veterans, their king was undergoing a strange metamorphosis: he was becoming an Oriental monarch.

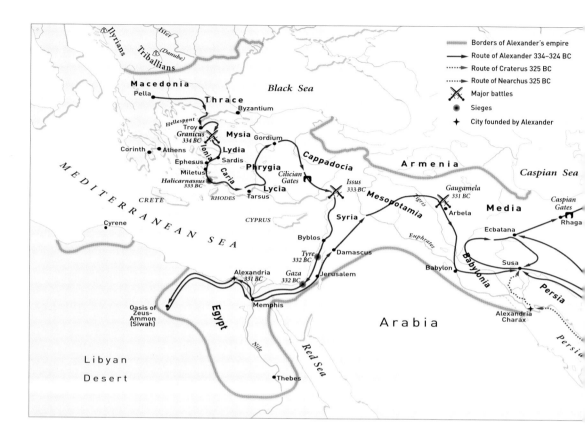

The most obvious changes involved ritual ceremonies, which to satisfy the new subjects had taken on important elements of Persian custom. With increasing frequency Alexander appeared in public wearing some of the opulent clothes of the Great King, even the high diadem, and carrying the royal seal. By far the most striking change was when

Plutarch

"It was in Parthia that he first put on the barbaric dress, perhaps with the view of making the work of civilizing them the easier, as nothing gains more upon men than a conformity to their fashions and customs. Or it may have been as a first trial, whether the Macedonians might be brought to adore as the Persians did their king, by accustoming them by little and little to bear with the alteration of his rule."

Alexander began to perform, first with his Oriental subjects and then with his Macedonians, the *proskynesis*, a deep bow followed by a hand gesture similar to blowing a kiss. This gesture, taken as ordinary by Asians, seemed ridiculous if not odious to the Hellenes, many of whom had no qualms about criticizing it openly. Among those most reluctant to accept such new customs were Philotas, Parmenion's son and commander of the cavalry, and the philosopher Callisthenes, champion of Greek culture. Within a few months, both met cruel ends. Philotas, whose popularity was beginning to overshadow even Alexander, was first. He was accused of having failed to immediately report a plot against Alexander after learning of it himself. Arrested, he was brought before an assembly that included numerous envious enemies. He tried to defend himself, calling the charges against him false, but the only one with the power to pardon

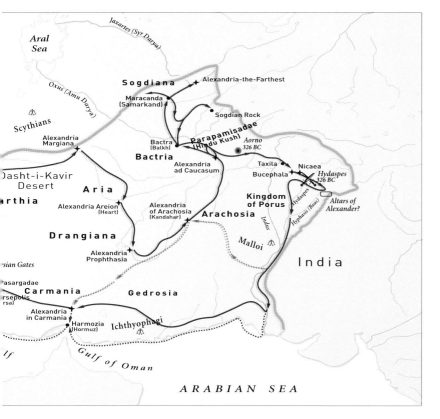

Left: Map giving the borders and size of the empire of Alexander the Great, extending from Greece to India. After conquering the Persian kingdoms, Alexander demonstrated great political intelligence in supporting the customs and traditions of his new subjects.

Below: The death of Perdiccas, marble relief from the Alexander Sarcophagus; Archaeological Museum, Istanbul.

him was Alexander, and his childhood friend did not want to listen. On the suggestion of Craterus, Philotas was tortured until he admitted his guilt, after which he was stoned to death. After his son's execution, the loyalty of Parmenion became doubtful, so Alexander, faced with the serious danger of a mutiny in his army, sent assassins to murder Parmenion. So it was that the man who had been one of the principal factors behind the success of both Philip and Alexander died at the age of seventy, stabbed by assassins. The message was clear, and the entire army understood it: from then on, criticizing Alexander could cost dearly.

The army was given new officers. Command of the cavalry was divided between Hephaistion and Cleitus; Craterus became vice-commander of the army. Coenus, the brother of the man who had organized the murder of Parmenion, assumed command of the infantry.

Despite the murders of Philotas and Parmenion, men who enjoyed great prestige among the soldiers, and although he was beginning to behave in ways that were hardly reassuring, Alexander did not lose any of his authority over his troops. In fact, he convinced the army to march on, across the impervious roads of central Asia to the satrapies of Aria and Drangiana. In the spring of 329 BC, he got his soldiers to cross the inaccessible Parapamisadae mountain range, today's Hindu Kush. They were always in pursuit of Bessus and his accomplices, or at least of those who had not had the good sense to surrender to the conqueror. While making his way forward, driven by his indomitable energy, Alexander continued to found cities, forty-two of which, according to tradition, eventually bore his name. Among these, all of them located on sites that were of strategic value, whether for military to trade reasons, were Alexandria Areion (now Herat), Alexandria Arachoton (now Kandahar), Alexandria-in-Sogdia (now Ai Khanum), and Alexandria ad Caucasum, to the north of Kabul. Veterans no longer fit for active service were settled in these places. Mixing with the indigenous populations, they spread the culture and civilization of their homeland in these remote areas. With his tireless vitality, Alexander was assuming superhuman dimensions in the eyes of his men, and aspects of the unknown regions they were crossing reminded them of scenes from mythology, giving them the illusion that they had found the cave of Prometheus, the Titan who had given men fire, or

were following the path taken by Hercules and Dionysus during their triumphal march eastward.

These military campaigns were also true journeys of exploration, for the geographers and scientists accompanying the soldiers collected detailed information on the climate, terrain, and flora and fauna of those mysterious lands. Their reports gave the West its first precise information concerning a broad swath of the Asian continent. Always eager to excel, Alexander was at the head of the column during marches, whether in desert sand or mountain snow. He shared his soldiers' hardships; if water was scarce he would refuse a cup offered only to him. He was there, swinging an ax to chop through the ice, opening a road for his men, and by his example he inspired those who were weary or discouraged to continue.

In Aria, Alexander put to flight the troops of Satibarzanes in a battle in which the traitorous satrap fell on the field. Then, continuing his pursuit of the assassins of Darius, Alexander penetrated Bactria, outflanking or assaulting the passes blocked by the followers of Bessus. Having passed the mountains, Alexander marched on without encountering further resistance until reaching Bactra, the capital of the satrapy, located at a fertile oasis. At that point the self-named Artaxerxes V was forced to take flight again. He crossed the Oxus, a wide river running along the edge of a rocky desert almost fifty miles wide, and took shelter in Sogdiana. In his desperate flight he gave orders for the destruction of all the bridges and boats in his rear, but Alexander, making use of the tried-and-true expedient of filling tent skins with hay to make rafts, succeeded in crossing the river. At that point Bessus met the same fate as the king whose throne he had usurped. When it became clear to those around him that he was powerless to oppose the invaders, he too was abandoned by his army and his Scythian allies. Handed over to his adversary, he was treated with barbaric ferocity. He was made to march naked and chained before the army, whipped and bleeding. His ears and nose were mutilated, and he was sent to Ectabana to be tried, and later condemned to death, by an assembly of Iranian nobles. Once again, Alexander had chosen to behave as a Persian monarch, unleashing his

Opposite: Oriental personage traveling on a camel in a red-figure vase painting from the fifth-fourth century BC; British Museum, London.

Above: Silver rhyton from Iran, fourth century BC; Museo Nazionale d'Arte Orientale, Rome.

Alexander, Between Orient and Occident

The death of Darius III represents a decisive moment in Alexander's personal and political world. Before then the Macedonian king had always behaved as a paragon of Greek virtues, dedicated to avenging the wrongs suffered by Greeks at the hands of the Persians. Before the lifeless body of his enemy, his behavior changed radically.

The empire he had hoped to punish was now his, but to preserve it he had to come to terms with the traditions that were at its base. The first changes began immediately. The king, who had already opened himself to Oriental customs by admitting the eunuch Bagoas among his intimates, began receiving his new Iranian subjects dressed in Persian style: white-and-red-striped tunic, purple sash, and on his head the diadem formerly worn by the Great King. He invited his Companions and the other officers of the army to wear mantles decorated with purple, and to dress up their horses with elaborate Persian trappings. Some sources even claim that Darius's 365 concubines (one for each day of the Babylonian year) were reinstated in their positions, and the life at Alexander's court increasingly displayed the influence of Asian ceremonies.

All these innovations were looked upon by the veterans with stupor followed by poorly veiled hostility. Unable to understand the political necessity of such gestures, the rough Macedonians soon judged them as signs of the arrogance and corruption of Alexander.

Cortege of dignitaries, relief from the stairs of the Apadana Palace, Persepolis.

tremendous wrath on the man who had betrayed Darius. Later, the last of the plotters, Barsentes, who had sought refuge in India, also fell into the hands of the Macedonians.

REVOLTS AND CONSPIRACIES

Still, the conquest could not be considered complete. Indeed, the defeat of Bessus marked the beginning of a new phase of difficult encounters in which success often proved fleeting and the efforts to subdue the region seemed hopeless. Yet even this new phase began with what seemed like ideal omens. Alexander easily took possession of Sogdiana, entering it without a battle, and also Marcanda (today's Samarkand), arriving on the banks of the Jaxartes River, which the Macedonians took for the Tanais (the Don), meaning the river that marked the border between Europe and Asia. On those banks Alexander planned to found Alexandria-the-Farthest, the city that would mark the northernmost border of his empire, beyond which stretched a frontier inhabited only the proud nomadic Scythian tribesmen, a people

no one had ever succeeded in subduing. But before work could begin on Alexandria-the-Farthest, news arrived that a revolt had broken out in Sogdiana, led by an aristocratic Persian named Spitamenes. Playing upon the anger caused by requisitions and the plundering carried out by the Macedonian army, Spitamenes had been able to wage ruthless guerrilla warfare. At the head of a small group of select horsemen, he struck isolated garrisons only to skillfully elude pursuit by taking refuge in the desert. Used to fighting it out in open fields, the Macedonians were ill prepared to deal with this type of warfare. Alexander's response was the formation of flying squads, compact units of mobile troops authorized to pillage. In his attempt to put down the insurrection, he also ordered attacks on the nomads on the opposite banks of the Jaxartes, the river that marked the border between the world of settled peoples and the tribes of the steppe. By doing so, he hoped to demonstrate to his enemies that there were no longer any secure hiding places. Although Alexander was seriously wounded in a skirmish, his attack was successful,

Left: Procession of Scythians (Saka) bearing gifts in a bas-relief from the Apadana Palace, Persepolis.

Above: Fragment of a sword and handle in the Scythian-Achaemenid style, from 500–400 BC; Hermitage, St. Petersburg.

Opposite top: Dying warrior, from the eastern pediment of the temple of Athena Aphaia at Aegina.

Opposite bottom: Gold belt plaque, Scythian art; Hermitage, St. Petersburg.

and many Scythian kings, frightened by the Macedonian catapults and ballistae, sent envoys to offer friendship. This did nothing to put a stop to Spitamenes. In one of his raids the Persian massacred an entire detachment of more than 2,000 Macedonians along the Politimetus (Zarafshan) River. It was the first defeat of Alexander's troops since the beginning of the expedition.

The event must have created a great deal of anxiety among Alexander's men, even among his closest friends, some of whom felt increasingly distant from him, particularly as his behavior grew more and more incomprehensible. At Maracanda, in the fall of 328 BC, the situation dramatically exploded. In the course of one of the usual drunken banquets that Alexander offered his friends and officers, a quarrel broke out. The subject of the dispute was the value of the veterans of King Philip: Alexander claimed they were inferior to the warriors of the new generations. Cleitus, who aside from being a longtime friend of Alexander had saved his life at the Grancius, took offense and defended the veterans, moving on to rail against the new rituals and declaring that the expedition's success was more the result of the courage shown by the soldiers than of that shown by Alexander. Drunk from wine, as happened more and more often, Alexander grabbed a spear from the hands of a nearby guard and ran it through his friend. When he later came to his senses, Alexander was distraught at what he had done and tried to commit suicide, being prevented from doing so by the intervention of friends. Many days were needed before he overcame the weight of his guilt, comforted all the while by the unshakable faith of his men.

Spitamenes had meanwhile continued his raids, but time was running out for him. After an assault in Bactria, in course of which he wiped out the garrison of the fortress of Zariaspa, the rebel was engaged and put to flight by the troops of Craterus. A short while later he was soundly defeated by Coenus, the courageous leader of the Macedonian infantry. The followers of the rebel were routed and dispersed. As a sign of peace, the Scythian horsemen who had taken part in the raids cut off Spitamenes's head and sent it to Alexander. The last, desperate attempt of the Persians to free themselves of the invaders had failed.

For Alexander, the moment had come to begin construction of a lasting empire. In doing so, he intended to concentrate on the fusion of the conquerors and the conquered. His was a farsighted plan, and it would have to overcome strong resistance, most of all from the Macedonians. As usual, Alexander was driven by unwavering convictions and was tenacious in the pursuit of his goals. His

biographers point out that his first act was motivated more by passion than by logical reasoning. Early in the spring of 327 BC, Alexander decided to leave his winter camp and finally take control of the mountains in eastern Sogdiana, where the population had still not surrendered. Although his enemies were hardly numerous, this was not an easy campaign. The weather was still inclement, and snow and cold decimated the Macedonian soldiers. The Sogdian rebels took refuge in an apparently impregnable fortress in the middle of the mountains and believed themselves safe. During a parley with some of them, the rebels taunted Alexander, saying that to take the fortress he would need soldiers with wings. Alexander, who was never fond of being mocked, offered great rewards to the first soldier to scale the peak behind the fortress. Three hundred Macedonian soldiers stepped forward and were supplied with ropes and tent pegs for the climb. With the skills of true alpine troops they reached the peak at the established hour. At that point the Sogdian rebels, distressed at the sight of enemies that had achieved the impossible, surrendered, and their leader, the Sogdian baron Oxyartes, offered Alexander a banquet. Among those

present was his daughter, named Roxane, Persian for "little star," a young girl of extraordinary beauty. With the exception of Barsine, Alexander had always shown a preference for homosexual love, but he fell in love with this girl and asked to marry her. The marriage had obvious political ramifications. By his example, which he invited his officers to emulate, Alexander intended to promote a very real union of the defeated and the victors.

Above: *Wedding of Alexander and Roxane,* eighteenth-century fresco by Giambattista Crosato.

Opposite top: Gold comb with battle scene,

Scythian art; Hermitage, St. Petersburg.

Opposite bottom: Alexander battling the Scythians, from the fifteenth-century book *Khamse,* by Nezami.

Quintus Curtius Rufus

"In this way the king of Asia and of Europe took to himself in wedlock a woman who had been brought in among the entertainments of a banquet, intending to beget from a captive a son who should rule over victors."

Alexander took several other moves to achieve his intention. Oxyartes, having become Alexander's father-in-law, was placed among the high Macedonian officials, while his sons entered elite units of the army. By then Alexander's army was rapidly losing its original characteristics. Alongside the Macedonian troops and the few remaining Greek mercenaries, there were large units from Bactria and Sogdiana. Alexander also gave the order to choose 30,000 boys from the region and give them training

in Macedonian ways. At court, the Macedonian and Iranian nobles were treated more often as equals, and the ceremonies were taking on increasingly Asian characteristics. Until then the Macedonian opposition to this trend had taken the form of a mute indignation, but now it was openly expressed through the mouth of Callisthenes, the cousin of Aristotle. The historian, who had been among the most obsequious adulators of Alexander, refused to prostrate himself before Alexander, proclaiming it unworthy of a free citizen of Hellas. This unexpected behavior was a bitter blow to Alexander, and from that moment on he greatly resented Callisthenes. A short time later a new plot was discovered, known as the Royal Pages' Conspiracy because it had been hatched by one of the royal pages seeking revenge for having been whipped for having broken court etiquette, spearing an animal during a hunt before Alexander (Persian etiquette called for the king to be granted the first shot). The boy had conceived a plan to eliminate the king, whom he and several other pages looked upon as a tyrant. Arrested together with his accomplices, the page mentioned the name of Callisthenes, who had been his teacher, saying he had been the moral inspiration for the plot. Thus was Alexander offered the chance to strike down the historian without risking the disapproval of those in his entourage who still admired and respected the man. The historian was arrested and probably ended his days in prison. This event marked an incurable break between Alexander and his old master Aristotle, who broke off all contact with the ruler of Asia.

Alexander's behavior on this and other occasions awakened indignation in his early biographers. Today, however, other considerations must be taken into account in reaching a judgment. For example, it cannot be ignored that Callisthenes, much like Aristotle, was a fanatical believer in the superiority of Greeks over all "barbarous" peoples; according to this opinion, such peoples were fit only to be subjects of the Greeks. Without doubt, Alexander's policy of promoting the basic equality of the conquered and the conquerors—even

though achieved using brutal methods and designed to increase his personal power—was fundamentally wiser and more advanced, aside from being destined to bear more enduring fruit. Alexander's daring plan, so disliked by the Macedonians and the continental Greeks, offended by what they saw as a betrayal of the Hellenistic cause, was fully understood and embraced by the Greeks of Asia Minor, who had been mixing with the surrounding peoples for centuries. They were thus the first to share Alexander's dream.

Left: Remains of the long colonnade to the south of the courtyard of the palace of Ai Khanum. The city, once known as Alexandria-in-Sogdia, was founded immediately after the death of Spitamenes.

Opposite top: Alexander-Zeus with Poseidon and Hercules in a marble relief from the Flavian age found in 1816 at Vigna Moroni near Rome; Antiquarium Romanum, Museo Gregoriano Etrusco, Rome.

Opposite bottom: Iron sword of 336 BC found at Vergina on the funeral pyre of the Macedonian King Philip II. Macedonian horseman used such weapons.

As it was, new and fascinating perspectives were soon to open for everyone. Having pacified the regions on the northeastern border, Alexander was seized by the irrepressible desire to go beyond all human limitations and follow to its conclusion his plan to dominate all of Asia, driving on to the farthest ends of the world. The new objective was India, a land that had known Persian rule only formally. The desire to move in that direction had long excited Alexander's mind, and he had been in contact with several rulers of the region, accepting their gifts. The plan remained vague, however, primarily because of scarce geographical information. Alexander, whose education had been based on the highly incomplete geographical notions of the period, was convinced that the lands that extended between the Indus and the shore of the ocean were relatively limited. According to the most widely accepted theories, the Punjab was a peninsula extending toward the southern ocean, perhaps even reaching the African continent. Some hypothesized that one could enter Egypt directly from the Punjab, thus completing a circular journey. The march to India was thus destined to be transformed into a true journey of discovery.

From the diplomatic and strategic points of view, the expedition was prepared in detail: diplomatic ties were made with the closest rulers and the troops were reorganized. The army was made more mobile and reinforced with massive Iranian contingents armed with spears along with units of horsemen. Some units, in particular the Shield Bearers, were given splendid new armor and silver shields, the magnificence of which could not fail to amaze enemies. The undertaking, which was to assure Alexander possession of the eastern ends of the inhabited world, would be grandiose in every respect.

To the Ends
of the World

Ruler of the empire of Darius, Alexander dreamed of extending his conquests to the far ends of the world, but the rebellion of his soldiers and a mysterious disease put an end to his undertaking, casting him into the universe of myth.

TOWARD A MYSTERIOUS LAND

Alexander's army set off in the late spring of 327 BC. According to ancient histories, this moving mass numbered no fewer than 120,000 people, between warriors (mostly Asian), women, children, traders, and all sorts of camp followers: an entire people in movement. On leaving Bactra, this multitude first turned southward, again crossing the chain of the Hindu Kush. To make the passage easier, Alexander had all superfluous material burned, including the carts that carried the spoils. He set the example himself by burning his own baggage. His men went along without rebelling, a clear sign that he had lost none of his influence with them. Following their passage, made easier by fine weather, Alexander decided to spend a few months at Alexandria-in-the-Caucasus. Here local recruits further reinforced the ranks of the army, already decidedly multiethnic. When it came time to set off, Alexander divided the army into two columns. One part of the troops, under the command of Perdiccas and Hephaistion, was to take the bulk of the baggage train and head toward the valley of the Indus River. It was to cross the Khyber Pass, the main access route to India, and keep open the lines of communication while also collecting provisions. The troops under the direct command of Alexander were to head toward the northern valleys, in the regions of Nuristan and Swat. The populations in that area put up a ferocious resistance to invasion, and the Macedonian army had to fight its way ahead. Presenting great difficulties, the campaign dragged on for nearly six months. The locals often retreated to a stronghold

and prepared to face siege. To put an end to such resistance, Alexander showed no pity and had large numbers of the defenders and inhabitants massacred. In the lands of the Assaceni, Alexander violated pacts and ordered the slaughter of several thousand Indian mercenaries who had surrendered and had been taken into his ranks but then had tried to escape. With the Nysa, he was instead very generous, in large part because he was convinced that their city was sacred to Dionysus, the divinity worshiped by his mother, Olympias. Here the Macedonians stopped to offer sacrifices and have banquets, happy to have found something in those distant regions that reminded them so much of home. In all probability, the cult the Greeks interpreted as being related to Dionysus was directed at the Hindu god Shiva. The next stop was the citadel of Aornos, a fortified mountain that, according to legend, not even the demigod Hercules had succeeded in conquering. The undertaking was thus a challenge to Alexander, and he began the siege determined to prove himself superior to his mythical ancestor. Having first sent Ptolemy with a small contingent to occupy and fortify some high ground nearby, Alexander led the advance at the head of his tough Macedonian highlanders and the Agrianians, crossing ravines and gorges and building fortified mounds from which the Macedonian artillery targeted the citadel with ballistae and catapults. During the final assault,

Opposite: Site of the ancient city of Bazira (now Barikot), conquered by Alexander (Swat, Pakistan).

Above: Copper knife and iron lance head, fifth to sixth century BC, from the tombs of the necropolis of Katelai at Swat (Pakistan); Museo Nazionale d'Arte Orientale, Rome.

Below: Capital of pilaster strip in green schist, from Butkara, Swat (Pakistan).

Alexander personally led his scalers, who penetrated the fortress, destroying its defenses. Once again, the genius of Alexander and the strength of his troops seemed to have overcome the limits of the possible, carrying them into the realm of myth.

In truth, a sense of the legendary tinged every aspect of that journey. The exotic atmosphere of the lands being crossed—places of which little or nothing was known—made the march increasingly exciting and unreal. Alexander was seen as a new Dionysus, victoriously traveling the world. In their encounter with that unknown territory the Greeks drew on images from their mythology, interpreting what they encountered in the light of their cultural baggage.

In the spring of 326 BC, having first guaranteed the security of the newly conquered regions, entrusting them to faithful veterans, Alexander met up with the troops of Perdiccas and Hephaistion, already camped on the banks of the Indus River.

A New and Dangerous Adversary

The two generals had already built a bridge of boats across the river, and the army now used this to cross over and enter the lands of Taxila. Like those of several other nearby regions, the rajah had already been in contact with Alexander for quite some time, assuring him of military support in exchange for help in the war he was waging against nearby kings. True to his promises, the rajah now proclaimed himself a vassal to the Macedonian, sending provisions and assistance and welcoming the foreigner to his capital, Taxila. In this kingdom, the Greeks had their first encounters with several strange local customs. They saw men with dyed beards and linen tunics, protected from the sun by parasols; they met fakirs, Hindu sages, and perhaps also some Buddhist masters (although Alexander's soldiers interpreted Buddha as a member of the following of Dionysus). The Greeks were astonished by certain customs, such as widows throwing themselves on their husbands' funeral pyres and cadavers left exposed to dogs and vultures. Thirsty for new knowledge, Alexander sent one of his men, Onesicritus, who had studied with the great Cynic philosopher Diogenes, to talk with certain sages who gave lessons in the nude under the scorching sun. The conversation was quite difficult, both because the interpreters were not up to their task and because Onesicritus interpreted everything through the filter

Above: Alexander receives an Indian delegation in Versailles; fresco by Jean-Baptiste de Champaigne (1631–1684).

Opposite left: Cymbal player, fragment from Butkara;

Museo Nazionale d'Arte Orientale, Rome.

Opposite right: Statue of Buddha, second to third century BC; Museo Nazionale d'Arte Orientale, Rome.

of his preconceptions. We know, however, that the leader of these masters praised Alexander, calling him a "philosopher in arms," and that one of the sages, whom the Greeks called Calanus, was so intrigued by these newcomers that he joined Alexander's retinue. Over the next two years the venerable ascetic gave lessons to all the officers interested in his teachings and was looked upon fondly by Alexander himself. But India was not only a strange land in which one met fakirs, war elephants, and rivers swarming with fish and crocodiles. Alexander was also to come up against some of the most valiant warriors he had ever faced, along with many unexpected dangers against which his great intellect and his experience would not always prove sufficient. The reality of the situation became immediately clear when Alexander moved against the enemies of Taxila: Abisares, king of Kashmir, and most of all the warlike Porus, rajah of Paurava.

Alexander had asked both for their tribute and submission, but while Abisares had quickly sent emissaries to discuss treaties, Porus, a noble ruler and proud man, made it known to Alexander that his only tribute would be armed men. A battle was thus inevitable.

The rajah put great care into his preparations for the battle, assembling an enormous army along with hundreds of chariots and well-trained war elephants. He deployed this force in a very strong position along the banks of the broad Hydaspes River and there awaited the arrival of the invaders. To overcome this new challenge, Alexander made use of all his imagination as a strategist. He aligned his men on the opposite side of the river and ordered his officers to simulate attacks by day and night, marching in arms up and down the banks, blowing

The Battle of Hydaspes

The battle on the Hydaspes River (today's Jhelum) was Alexander's last major battle. His adversaries were not Persians, many of whom in fact fought in his army, but rather the Indian troops of the rajah of Paurava, Porus. Having rejected every invitation to submit to Alexander, Porus had assembled a large army, including war carts and more than two hundred elephants, on the left bank of the river, and there he awaited Alexander's arrival. Alexander misled Porus's troops with diversions and false alarms and outflanked them by fording the river at a place to the north. The crossing was not without problems; only when they had already sent back the boats used in the crossing did the Macedonians

realize they were on an island in the middle of the river, not the opposite shore. They were forced to swim to the far shore of the river. Arriving on his enemy's flank, Alexander advanced with archers and cavalry at the gallop, followed by infantry. The Macedonians were spotted by the Indian advance guard, but overran this initial resistance, killing the son of Porus. Only then did the rajah move the bulk of his force, aligning his troops to face Alexander's along a vast front, with the elephants in the front line and the cavalry and war carts on the flanks, ready to encircle the Greeks. Alexander reorganized his ranks and quickly took the initiative. Leaving the phalanx and Shield Bearers at the center to stop the elephants, he attacked Porus's left wing. The Persian mounted archers killed the drivers of the carts, and Alexander and his men charged the cavalry. At that point Porus sent all his cavalry to stop Alexander

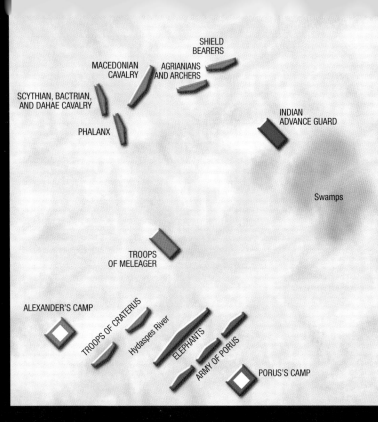

SHIELD BEARERS

MACEDONIAN CAVALRY

AGRIANIANS AND ARCHERS

SCYTHIAN, BACTRIAN, AND DAHAE CAVALRY

PHALANX

INDIAN ADVANCE GUARD

Swamps

TROOPS OF MELEAGER

ALEXANDER'S CAMP

TROOPS OF CRATERUS

Hydaspes River

ELEPHANTS

ARMY OF PORUS

PORUS'S CAMP

This was exactly what Alexander had been expecting. Ceoenus, waiting on the other end of the formation, went into action with a thousand horsemen, attacking the rear of the Indian cavalry, which fell into the trap. The rajah tried to intervene with his elephants, but the Macedonian infantry held up to the devastating charge of the elephants, using arrows and sarissas to unseat the drivers and wound the animals, which went out of control and ended up trampling their own troops. The Indian army became a confused mass of elephants, men, and horses surrounded by the Macedonian cavalry and pressed from every side by the ranks of the phalanx and Shield Bearers. A fearless warrior and powerful man, Porus battled to the end, firing arrows from the back of his enormous war elephant, but in the end, seriously wounded, he had to retreat. The outcome of the battle had been decided. Even the troops of Craterus, which until then had stayed in place to hold down the enemy on the right flank, now crossed the river to join Alexander's pursuit of the fleeing enemy. The battle on the Hydaspes was the bloodiest of Alexander's victories. Having lost two-thirds of his army, Porus found himself forced to accept Alexander's terms and become his vassal.

horns, and making suitable noises. The Indian troops had to respond to each of these false alarms, forming defensive ranks and keeping alert, and over time this wearied them and made them lower their guard—which is what Alexander had been waiting for. Leaving a large contingent under Craterus with orders to continue the false alarms of attack, Alexander got his chosen troops to the other side, crossing the river about sixteen miles upriver of the camp. When Porus realized what was happening, he first sent an advance guard led by his son against the Greeks and followed it with the bulk of his troops. The battle that took place was one of the most violent that Alexander fought. The Macedonian veterans, the infantry in particular, had to defend themselves from the onslaught of hundreds of charging elephants. They were successful. Unlike Darius, Porus fought to the end and only then, badly wounded, did he ask to be brought before Alexander. The meeting between the two noble, courageous adversaries was chivalric. Alexander accepted the submission of the rajah and not only reconfirmed him ruler of his lands but added some of the surrounding territory to his dominions. The decision proved wise, for from then on Porus was Alexander's strongest and most faithful ally in the area. After the battle of Hydaspes, which was to be his last large battle, Alexander founded two cities: Nicaea, the City of Victory, and Bucephala, named in

honor of his glorious warhorse, soon to die of old age. He then gave the order to build a gigantic river fleet. He planned to have this fleet descend the Indus, the river that many, in the light of the sketchy geographical knowledge of the time, believed to be an upper branch of the Nile. The presence of crocodiles in its waters seemed to confirm this hypothesis. Alexander intended to take the bulk of his forces farther east, up to the very borders of the world. Of course, those borders keep moving farther into the distance. From the information the soldiers gathered while marching ahead, they realized their situation was far different from what they had imagined. First, they learned that the Indus emptied in an unknown ocean and that it had nothing to do with the Nile; then they heard about a vast plain that extended to the east and was crossed by an immense river

Quintus Curtius Rufus

"His desire for glory and insatiable thirst for fame did not let him see anything as impossible, anything as too far."

(the Ganges), on the banks of which lived a hostile people with elephants even larger and more ferocious than those of Porus. Far from being troubled by such news, Alexander looked forward to the next confrontation. A superhuman undertaking like the conquest of all Asia could and should have a heroic dimension. He ordered his men to advance.

Above: *Alexander and Porus,* painted by Charles Le Brun, 1673; Louvre, Paris. Louis XIV was a great admirer of Alexander and had Le Brun make paintings of all of his exploits.

Right: Greek wellhead with scene of sacrifice; Vatican Museums, Rome.

Opposite: Painting of war elephants on a large plate dated to ca. 280 BC; Villa Giulia, Rome.

For the first time, his soldiers refused to carry out the order. To them, the situation had become unbearable. Monsoon rains, completely unknown to the Greeks, had transformed the Punjab into an expanse of swamps infested with poisonous snakes, and the march was made even more arduous by the continuous rain and the obstinate resistance of the locals. When they made it to the Hyphasis River (today's Beas), not far from Amritsar, the troops mutinied. Seated on the banks of the river under the pouring rain, the veterans of a hundred battles showed Alexander their wounds and, through the mouth of the valiant Coenus, begged him to halt the advance and turn around. After using all the arguments at his disposal to convince them to change

their minds, Alexander retired in anger to his tent and for three days refused to speak to anyone. In the end he came to his senses and, to the jubilation of his soldiers, reluctantly gave in to their request. Before beginning the retreat, Alexander gave orders to celebrate rites and to organize athletic competitions. Twelve enormous altars were erected and sacrifices were offered, giving thanks to the gods for the victories won. Alexander intended

Right: Alexander sailing toward the western sea in one of the six miniatures of the Indian manuscript *Divan* by Ali Sher Navai, compiled between 1526 and 1527; Bibliothèque Nationale, Paris.

Opposite top: Fragment of relief with quadriga from second century AD; Museo Nazionale d'Arte Orientale, Rome.

Opposite bottom: Bronze statuette of horse, first century BC, from Herculaneum; Museo Archeologico, Naples.

these altars, located at the far ends of the empire, to constitute eternal monuments to their accomplishment, but within the span of a few centuries the flooding of the Hyphasis had washed away all trace of them.

THE RETURN

Composed of about 80,000 men, the army now returned to the banks of the Hydaspes, where the construction of two thousand cargo boats and eighty-odd small warships was nearly complete. Command of this fleet was given to Nearchus, a Macedonian of Cretan birth, a childhood friend of Alexander and a leading figure in Alexander's general staff. At the

beginning of the expedition in India, Nearchus—statesman, soldier, and skilled navigator—had been summoned from the province of Lycia, of which he was satrap. The expedition's pilot was to be the Cynic philosopher Onesicritus. Having laid aside the fantastic plan of traveling all the way to Alexandria in Egypt, Alexander's army and fleet began descending toward the ocean. The ships on the river were flanked on both banks by troops commanded by Craterus and Hephaistion, who had the task of eliminating any pockets of resistance that might be encountered along the route. Navigating the river proved far less easy than foreseen and was not without dangers. At the confluence of the Hydapses with another river, the flagship ran the risk of sinking, and Alexander and his companions saved themselves by swimming. The hostility of the people of the southern Punjab was worse than expected. The population of the Malloi, in particular, turned out to be tremendously aggressive. Alexander punished these people, devastating their lands with the furor of a hurricane; he even ordered the complete extermination of all the Brahman priests, since these incited the people to war. The violent reaction of the indigenous peoples greatly diminished the enthusiasm of the troops, such that Alexander felt himself compelled to personally take over leadership of the operations. At the siege of the main fortress of the Malloi, Alexander was first over the wall, leaping down alone into the fort, where he found himself surrounded by enemies who attacked him from every side, firing arrows. Before his bodyguard had time to reach him and get him to safety, he had been hit by a long Indian arrow that went through his chest armor and pierced a lung. The wound was so serious that word of his death soon spread among his men, who were seized by panic, fully aware that they had little hope of seeing their homes without their leader. Once again, however, Alexander's great physical strength saved him, and to the enormous relief of his men he slowly began to recover. The tribes of the Malloi were forced to submit, but there were still other enemies to face, the clashes continuing until they reached the area of the Indus delta.

There, Alexander divided his forces. The oldest and most experienced soldiers formed a column under the command of Craterus, with orders to head off toward the center of the empire following the easiest route, the one across Arachosia. Alexander would lead the bulk of the army westward toward Babylon, following the coast and flanked by the fleet commanded by Nearchus. After exploring both arms of the river delta, on one of which they founded a new city, they finally reached the ocean. There, Alexander and his men made the dramatic discovery of another phenomenon unknown to the inhabitants of the Mediterranean: the great ocean tides, which suddenly flooded the camp.

On those distant shores Alexander performed the sacrifices he had learned from the oracle of Siwah. He then sailed into the water to offer bulls to Poseidon. He poured libations into the water and also threw in the golden bowls and cups he had used, praying to the gods and asking that no other person be allowed to surpass what he had achieved on his expedition. With these rituals, similar to those performed years earlier on the Hellespont, Alexander hoped to create an ideal junction of the beginning and end of his expedition. At the same time, having realized that he was not sailing on an internal sea but on an ocean that, as far as was known, embraced all the inhabited land of the earth, he began to conceive a new ambition, that of dominating not only Asia, but all of the earth.

First, however, he would have to return to the heart of his kingdom, for troublesome news had been

Quintus Curtius Rufus

"Beginning my reign in Macedonia, I hold dominion over Greece, I have subdued Thrace and the Illyrians, I rule the Triballians and the Medi, I possess Asia from where it is washed by the Hellespont to the shores of the Red Sea."

New Geographical Discoveries

Alexander led his army across many regions that were unexplored, areas that were unknown in Greece or known only from partial or inexact reports. Fragments of information concerning those distant regions had been spread by such works as the texts of Aristotle and were often based on groundless rumors. And yet those very lands had been explored by a Greek, Scylax of Caryanda, not so long before. On orders from Darius I, this enterprising navigator had sailed along the coast of the Caspian Sea, discovering its nature as an internal sea; descending the Indus, he had then sailed into and explored the Persian Gulf. Scylax had left a detailed report of these voyages in Greek: Periplus of the Sea of Europe, Asia, and Libya.

A century and a half later, all memory of this undertaking had been forgotten. Thus, during his Indian journey the admiral Nearchus was forced to repeat from the beginning all the experiences of the earlier voyager. A scientist as well as a skilled navigator, Nearchus was the first Westerner to study the phenomenon of the oceanic tides and to understand how the monsoon winds could be used for travel on routes between the Orient and the Occident. Intrigued by these ideas, Alexander decided to send other exploratory expeditions into the Persian Gulf, the principal aim of which would be to collect useful information for the conquest of the entire Arabian peninsula. His sudden death put an end to the plans.

Above: Alexander traveling toward the land of the shadows in a miniature from an Indian manuscript of Khamse by Nezami, fifteenth century; Metropolitan Museum of Art, New York.

Left: Attic black-figure cup with images of Greek square-sailed galleys.

Opposite: Head of Alexander from Pergamum; Archaeological Museum, Istanbul.

reaching him concerning poor administration and corrupt satraps. Along the way he planned to complete the exploration of that part of the continent, opening new trade routes. At the end of the summer of 325 BC the army moved. Once again the undertaking had been planned with care. The most experienced troops, led by Alexander in person, were to cross the terrible sands of the Gedrosian desert, proceeding along the coast to the Persian Gulf. Along the way they were to dig wells and set up food deposits for the fleet, which was to sail from the mouth of the Indus to the mouth of the Euphrates and then ascend that river to Babylon. The difficulties to be faced were great.

Alexander intended to march an entire army over some of the most inhospitable and desolate terrain on the planet. Years earlier, those same arid expanses had seen the disaster of the armies led by Cyrus the Great, founder of the Persian Empire, and of Queen Semiramis. Only with difficulty had the two sovereigns escaped with their very lives.

To Alexander this was only one more of the many challenges he loved to take on to prove that for him nothing was impossible, but this time the conqueror had done his calculations poorly. As could have been foreseen, the march turned into a nightmare. The

army soon found itself forced to move away from the coastline to follow the only possible routes, those that led into the heart of the desert. Hunger, thirst, and the bites of poisonous snakes began to cut down hundreds of victims. One day the column, which had stopped on a nearly dry riverbed, was struck by a

sudden flood that swept away women, children, and baggage. Back on the arid, stony ground, the exhausted soldiers soon completely forgot the wells and food supplies they were supposed to establish for the sailors. They suffered terrible thirst in heat that was so great they could move only by night—

and even then the burning sand made the march painful. When, after sixty days of suffering, Alexander reached the capital of Gedrosia, only a fourth of his regular army, about 15,000 men, was still alive. No news had arrived of the fleet, which was believed lost, but Alexander consoled himself with the thought that he had outdone both Semiramis and Cyrus.

In Kerman, Alexander's force joined the column led by Craterus, and Alexander severely punished the satraps that had failed to send him help. They then began the march toward the center of the empire. At this point, Alexander had the march transformed into a Dionysian procession in which he himself took the role of the god making his triumphant return from the East. At the head of a cortege of festive soldiers, Alexander rode on a cart drawn by eight horses, on which was placed an altar. On this mobile stage Alexander spent the seven days and seven nights of the trip drinking wine, imitated by his

Above: *Alexander the Great's Entry into Babylon* (detail), marble frieze by Bertel Thorvaldsen, 1812; Palazzo del Quirnale, Rome.

Left: The desert region of the Sutkakh (Makran, Pakistan), in ancient Gedrosia, the region on the Indian Ocean that submitted to Alexander between 330 and 327 BC.

officers, who followed him aboard other sumptuous wagons. When they neared the Bay of Harmozia (today's Hormuz) the Greeks discovered that Nearchus and his sailors had survived. Alexander rushed to his old friend and warmly celebrated this unexpected reunion.

Despite having to face tremendous difficulties, the Cretan admiral had succeeded in completing his mission, procuring the necessary provisions and attacking encampments of the Ichthyophagi (fish-eaters), the primitive people that inhabited the coast.

The route the fleet had followed could not, as Alexander had hoped, become a regular trade route, but the discoveries made by Nearchus and his captains were of great value, in particular those concerning the Arabian peninsula, which in fact was for the first time discovered to be a peninsula. On Alexander's orders, Nearchus left with the ships with the intention of ascending the Tigris to Susa, while the rest of the troops set off for that city by land along the route that passed through Persepolis.

Quintus Curtius Rufus

"When I desired to propagate the stock of my race more extensively, I took to wife a daughter of Darius and set the example to my nearest friends of begetting children from captives, in order that by this sacred alliance I might abolish all distinction between vanquished and victor."

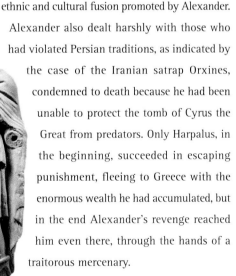

Right: The tomb of Cyrus the Great at Persepolis.

Below: Statute of a youth, perhaps Alexander, first century BC. The sculpture, in pale gray marble with light blue shading, was given to the museum of Athens in 1880 by the Archaeological Society, which had received it from the Dimitriou Collection of Alexandria, Egypt.

Opposite: Central portion of the Dionysus Mosaic of Pella. During his last years, Alexander showed great dedication to the god of wine, whose worship had been so important to his mother, Olympias.

THE LAST YEARS

The great expedition came to its conclusion in March of 324 BC. Alexander had conquered and explored an endless empire, pushing on to the ends of the inhabited world. His creation, however, proved to be fragile and insecure. Convinced that the king would never return from his expedition, many satraps, including several Macedonian administrators, had committed abuses and usurpations, setting themselves up as the autonomous rulers of their provinces. Even one of Alexander's oldest companions, the treasurer Harpalus, responsible for the administration of the royal treasury, had been guilty of misusing and squandering the funds, behaving like an independent lord, even assembling his own private army. To regain control of the empire, Alexander acted as usual with great determination. All the satraps that had rebelled or had failed in their duties were executed or removed, in many cases replaced by Macedonian generals who had shown they were more open to the plans of ethnic and cultural fusion promoted by Alexander. Alexander also dealt harshly with those who had violated Persian traditions, as indicated by the case of the Iranian satrap Orxines, condemned to death because he had been unable to protect the tomb of Cyrus the Great from predators. Only Harpalus, in the beginning, succeeded in escaping punishment, fleeing to Greece with the enormous wealth he had accumulated, but in the end Alexander's revenge reached him even there, through the hands of a traitorous mercenary.

After putting down these rebellions, Alexander dedicated himself to consolidating and reorganizing the state. He did this in part through a series of

Left: Alexander as Helios Cosmocrator, fragment of terra-cotta vase of the third to second century BC; Musée du Cinquanténaire, Brussels.

Opposite: Marriage of Alexander-Ares and Stateira-Aphrodite in a fresco from Pompeii.

Below: Weight in the shape of a lion, from Abydos, on the Dardanelles; British Museum, London.

symbolic ceremonies that once again served the purpose of confirming the union of Macedonians and Persians. The culmination of these celebrations was a lavish mass wedding ceremony in which Alexander and about one hundred of his closest associates married women belonging to the local high nobility. On this occasion, Alexander took two new wives: Stateira, daughter of his rival Darius III, and Parysatis, daughter of Darius's predecessor, Artaxerxes III. Alexander had his closest friend Hephaistion become his brother-in-law, giving him as wife another of Darius's daughters. The weddings of the other officials, who were thus joined to the Persian high society, were followed by those of about ten thousand Macedonian soldiers, who were effectively forced to officially marry the women they had brought with them from Sogdiana and Bactria.

It was Alexander's hope that the children of these unions would constitute the core of the future armed forces of the empire. These authoritarian dispositions were greeted with a certain repugnance by the soldiers, most of all the veterans of the phalanx. In response, Alexander pensioned off the veterans, replacing them with new recruits more willing to accept the creation of mixed units. Philip's old soldiers reacted with anger. Their protest was suppressed with the execution of the ringleaders and the granting of bonuses to those who agreed to return home. The task of escorting the old soldiers on their return trip was entrusted to the faithful Craterus, and Alexander also made him the governor of Macedonia, replacing the less-trusted Antipater. This decision was connected to Alexander's intention of extending to his European dominions the same style of Asian sovereignty he had made his own. To this end, Alexander had sent off a decree inviting the communities in the League of Corinth to include him among the divinities to whom they paid homage. Naturally, the rational citizens of Athens and the other cities, and even Antipater himself, responded to this order with extreme reluctance even if, for political reasons, they eventually obeyed. This was not Alexander's only decree to displease the Greeks. Not long afterward, in fact, he ordered all the cities of the league to permit all those who had been

Hephaistion, only recently named chiliarch, or grand vizier, fell ill and shortly afterward died. The death of his friend—and perhaps lover—deeply saddened Alexander, who fell into the most desperate manifestations of grief, including the massacre of an entire tribe of Iranians, killed as sacrificial victims. On the suggestion of the oracle of Siwah, whom Alexander had immediately consulted, the dead Hephaistion was accorded semidivine honors and a sepulchre of gigantic proportions was built in his memory. Ancient historians report that from then on Alexander was troubled by gloomy presentiments. This dark cloud accompanied him throughout the last months of his life but did not prevent him from going over his new plans of conquest with Nearchus and other generals. Some of these plans

banished during the civil conflicts to return home. This was a serious intrusion in the internal politics of the peninsula, which clearly showed how Alexander considered himself not just leader of the army, but the ruler of Hellas as well. Alexander was probably well aware of the fact that this imposition would awaken revolts and rebellions, but his interest in distant Greece was by then marginal. His main occupation now was that of reorganizing the new territories. He traveled constantly among the kingdom's various satrapies. Seated on his golden throne set up under a large tent covered with precious carpets, surrounded by generals and his Persian and Macedonian troops, Alexander meted out justice and dictated laws like a true Eastern sovereign. For him too, however, fate had in store bitter days.

In the fall of 324 BC, at the end of one of the drinking parties to which he and his companions abandoned themselves with increasing frequency,

Above: Colossal bronze head of Hephaistion, ca. 323 BC, probably from Pompeii or Herculaneum; it first belonged to Isabella d'Este, then to Philip V of Spain; Prado, Madrid.

Right: Statue of youth, probably representing Hephaistion, first century BC; Archaeological Museum, Athens.

Opposite top: *The Triumph of Alexander the Great,* painting by Gustave Moreau (1826–1898); Musée Moreau, Paris.

Opposite bottom: Calyx krater with painting by Euphronios depicting a banquet scene; Antikensammlungen, Munich.

were highly ambitious, such as one to circumnavigate Africa and return to the Mediterranean by way of the Pillars of Hercules, conquering Carthage along the way. Since not a single enemy existed capable of opposing him, Alexander, never satisfied with his conquests, clearly planned to conquer the entire world. To that end he planned a military operation for the conquest of Arabia, of which Nearchus had already explored the eastern coasts. Troops

suitable for combat in the desert were enlisted, and orders were given to build a new fleet that would descend along the Persian Gulf. Headquarters for this new operation were set up at Babylon, and Alexander moved there himself in the spring of 323 BC. This time, his arrival in the city coincided with a series of dark omens that were communicated to him by the Chaldean priests. Anxious to prove such predictions groundless, Alexander made every effort to appear active and

determined, even though he himself, according to his biographers, was obsessed by supernatural fears. At the end of May in 323 BC, after a feast involving the usual quantities of wine, Alexander fell ill. Treatments were lavished on him, sacrifices were offered to the gods, but his condition worsened. He suffered violent attacks of fever, likely a form of malignant malaria contracted during an inspection of the canals around Babylon. Plans for the voyage to Arabia were abandoned as he weakened.

By the end of the week, he could no longer speak and was barely able to nod at each of his soldiers,

Above: *The Death of Alexander the Great,* canvas painted by Karl Theodor Von Piloty; Bayerische Staatsgemäldesammlungen, Munich.

Below: Marble bust of the dying Alexander; Uffizi, Florence. Over the centuries, Alexander's sudden and mysterious death has inspired many artists.

Arrian

"Alexander died in the hundred and fourteenth Olympiad . . . he lived thirty-two years and eight months. He excelled in physical beauty, in zest for exertions, in shrewdness of judgment, in courage, in love of honor and danger, and in care for religion. . . . Anyone who reproaches Alexander should not do so by merely citing actions that merit reproach, but should collect all his actions together, and then carefully reflect . . . given what Alexander became and the height of human good fortune he attained, the unquestioned king of both continents whose name reached every part of the world."

who filed past him in a long line to pay homage. After giving Perdiccas the ring and seal symbolic of his power, Alexander lost consciousness, and three days later, on June 10, he died. He was not yet thirty-three years old.

THE SUCCESSORS

Alexander's empire outlived the death of its creator only briefly. With the loss of his commanding personality, the empire disintegrated. The conquered territories moved away from central control through a strong centrifugal force that led to increasingly autonomous policies of the Macedonian generals and administrators who succeeded Alexander. These generals and administrators are known to history as the Diadochi, Greek for "successors." When they assembled following the death of their king, the Macedonian commanders gave absolutely no consideration to the fact that Roxane was pregnant with the legitimate heir to Alexander; they also discarded his illegitimate son, Heracles, born to his

---

Suspicions Regarding a King's Death

Since antiquity, Alexander's sudden death and the fact that it took place under such ambiguous circumstances—when he was in the prime of life and at the height of his glory—has led to suspicions of a crime. At the time, rumor had it that Antipater, about to be replaced by Craterus as Alexander's lieutenant in Macedonia, had ordered one of his sons to poison Alexander. According to some versions, the assassin, perhaps Iollas, Alexander's cupbearer, used arsenic in its native state, taken from the silver-bearing galena of Macedonian mines; it had been his brother, Cassander, future murderer of the royal family, who had brought the poison to Babylon, hidden inside a box carved from the hoof of a mule. Most modern scholars lean in favor of disease and advance various possibilities: leukemia, cerebral abscess, or cirrhosis of the liver caused by the abuse of wine: by the time of his death Alexander was drinking five to six liters every night. The most probable cause, which is confirmed by what can be deduced about the course of the illness from the ancient biographers, is a lethal attack of malaria caused by the parasite Plasmodium falciparum, *an endemic disease around Babylon with a rapid course for which at the time there was no cure.*

Above: Mold with head of Alexander, ca. 300 BC, from the Acropolis of Heraclea in Lucania, southern Italy.

Right: Elegant silver cup found in the tomb of Philip at Vergina.

Persian mistress Barsine. As new monarch they chose instead the only surviving Argead: Arrhidaeus, Alexander's mentally retarded half-brother, with Craterus becoming his guardian. But the death of Alexander unleashed the very worst instincts in many people. In the span of only a few months, Roxane disposed of Alexander's new wives by having them poisoned, and a continuous series of mutinies and rebellions broke out among the soldiers and officers. The designated heir, Perdiccas, was murdered

by his own guards. Craterus died in battle while attempting to hold together Alexander's conquests. There followed years of wars and assassinations on a vast scale. The veterans of a thousand battles slaughtered one another in bloody fratricidal struggles until the empire was finally divided up. Ptolemy took control of Egypt, to Seleucus went the region around Babylon, Antigonus took Asia Minor and Syria, Lysimachus, one of Alexander's former bodyguards, got Thrace, and Cassander, the son of Antipater, ruled Macedonia and Greece. Even dismembered, the empire would be tormented by decades of continuous conflicts, in the course of which all of Alexander's family was eventually swept away. The indomitable Olympias, having had

Arrhidaeus and a hundred of Cassander's friends and relatives killed, was in turn defeated and killed by Cassander. He then went after Roxane and her son, named Alexander IV; both were imprisoned and then murdered. The next year, with the death of Heracles, who died under mysterious circumstances, the conqueror's dynasty became extinct.

THE MYTH OF ALEXANDER

In historical reality, Alexander's death was immediately followed by the fragmentation of his empire and the end of his political goals. In terms of myth, however, Alexander and the epic tale of his exploits met a far different destiny, their fame increasing and enduring over the centuries. Not even great Roman emperors, such as Julius Caesar and his nephew Augustus, were to escape this spell, and both of them went to Alexandria in Egypt to reverently visit the great leader's tomb. In reality, the legend of Alexander was beginning to take shape even while he was still alive, and some aspects of it were spread quite purposefully, beginning with that of his "divine" origin.

After his death, the figure of the Macedonian was transformed into a true incarnation of human glory and power. This operation had begun at the hands of historians who accompanied Alexander on his journey and whom Alexander himself sometimes took to task for their exaggerations. He was not pleased to find himself the author of such incredible undertakings as the slaughter of rows of elephants with a single thrust of his spear or encounters with Amazons and other fantastic beings. The stories based on nothing more than pure and simple adulation were soon joined by others dreamed up to serve political ends. In *Romance of Alexander,* a text groundlessly attributed to Callisthenes and written in an Egyptian setting, Alexander is said to have been born from the adulterous relationship between Olympias and the

pharaoh Nectanebo, sorcerer and necromancer; all of this with the intention of joining Alexander to the last indigenous dynasty of Egypt. In the same way, some Iranian traditions attribute the paternity of Alexander to the Great King. The figure of the young, undefeated leader who died in the full splendor of his glory evidently inspired the writers who recounted his exploits to shift him into the realm of myth. Even the sharp-witted Plutarch, who dedicated part of his *Parallel Lives* to Alexander, although suspicious of all things related to superstition and the miraculous, ended up creating the portrait of a superhuman personality who had revealed aspects of his future greatness even as an infant. Since the most reliable reconstructions of Alexander's life, such as that by Ptolemy, which were based on the original document of the expedition, have been lost, the historian must today turn to the surviving works of Quintus Curtius Rufus, Justin, and most of all Arrian. Some readers still prefer the fantastic tales presented in the book by the Pseudo-Callisthenes. In *Romance of Alexander,* Alexander moves between marvels and omens, confronting monsters, angels, and strange hybrid beasts. His trip, full of initiation rites, brings him to crystal castles, to the bottom of the sea in a transparent submarine, even up into the sky, carried by griffons. In this way, Alexander became symbolic of the human struggle to overcome the limitations to which humanity is subject, including even death, which in *Romance* he tries to defeat by drawing on the well of immortality.

Opposite: Portrait bust of Seleucus I; Museo Archeologico, Naples.

Right: Gypsum tablet from the third century BC with portrait of Ptolemy I, from the quarter of Hellenic artisans of Memphis. Following Alexander's death in 323 BC, Ptolemy administered Egypt as satrap, assuming the title of king in 305 BC.

Hellenistic Civilization

From the political point of view, Alexander's creation led to no enduring results, since his vast empire rapidly broke up into different states often battling among themselves. From the cultural point of view, however, Alexander's achievements enjoyed extraordinary fecundity. During the period following his death the entire eastern Mediterranean area experienced exceptional economic and artistic growth. Alexander's dream of spreading the language and culture of Greece to all the territories he had conquered led to the birth of a new civilization, which has come to be known to history under the name Hellenism, a term coined by the German historian Johann Gustav Droysen. The period of the Hellenistic civilization was distinguished by the decline of the old city-state system, replaced by strong, centralized monarchies based on the figure of deified rulers supported by standing armies and massive bureaucracies. The major cities of such kingdoms became grand metropolises, such as Pergamum, Antioch, and Alexandria, which became populous international marketplaces and centers of refined artistic production. The free flow of ideas, favored by the common language (the *koine*, which replaced the earlier Greek dialects), led to new discoveries, most of all in theoretical science. Aristarchus of Samos was first to propose a heliocentric theory of the universe; Archimedes revolutionized hydrostatics and mechanics; Apollonius of Perga gave an important impulse to geometry and Erasistratus to medicine. In literature, Apollonius Rhodius brought the epic back to popularity and Callimachus and Theocritus gave life to new and refined forms of poetry. Along with administrative activities, Alexandria and Pergamum created public museums and libraries such as had never before been seen. These prodigious institutions favored the activity of collecting and commenting on ancient texts, making possible the preservation of many works that have reached us. The growth of this cosmopolitan society, with its munificent rulers, also led to the spread of new ideas in city planning and the visual arts, characterized by a decided taste for the grandiose and the dramatic. A typical masterpiece of this period is the famous altar of Pergamum, the imposing frieze of which steals the scene from the architectonic

structure, which is reduced to a purely supportive role. The Hellenistic period also saw great development in the fields of sculpture and painting, which aside from the "glorified" portraits of Alexander made from life by the sculptor Lysippos and the painter Apelles (all of which are sadly lost) eventually arrived at a "baroque" art that preferred the most dramatic subjects, rich in pathos, such as the splendid *Laocoön* group or the *Punishment of Dirce.*

Left: The altar of Zeus at Pergamum, built by Eumenes II around 180 BC and reconstructed in the Staatliche Museen, Berlin.

Below: *Laocoön and His Sons,* marble sculpture from the second century BC; Vatican Museums, Rome.

The Burial of Alexander the Great

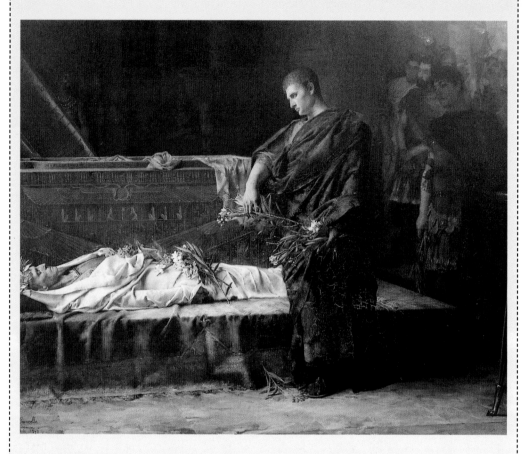

Following Alexander's death, discord broke out among his generals so quickly that the great leader's corpse was neglected for six days in the torrid climate of Babylon. When someone finally found the time to look after the body, it was discovered to be miraculously intact, and once they had overcome their misgivings about touching a god, the Egyptian and Chaldean embalmers were able to prepare it, covering it in perfumes. In life, Alexander had expressed the wish to be buried in the oasis of Siwah in the sanctuary of Ammon. For political reasons, the generals decided to move the coffin to Macedonia, using an elaborate funeral cart drawn by sixty-four mules. Ptolemy intercepted the cortege and convinced the officer in charge to take the body instead to Alexandria, capital of his new kingdom. There, in one of the catacombs reserved for his family, he arranged an ornamental sepulchre for his former commander in which the incorruptible body of the conqueror could be viewed through a sarcophagus of transparent alabaster. Over the course of the numerous wars that shook Egypt in the Middle Ages, the sepulchre was buried in rubble, its location forever lost.

Caesar at the Tomb of Alexander, painted by Gustave Courtois, 1878; Musée de Vesoul, Paris.

With the passage of centuries, *Romance of Alexander* went through many versions, both in the West and the East, where it was translated in all the languages of Alexander's ephemeral empire and also in those of the regions that Alexander never reached, up to the true borders of Asia. With every new translation the book took on new tones, and Alexander, too, changed, assuming different characteristics, sometimes presented as a knightly paladin of justice, truth, and wisdom. The legend became widespread in the Iranian and Muslim world. Under the name Dhu al-Qarnayn, the "two-horned" (probably derived from the two horns of the god Ammon with which he was presented on coins),

Alexander appears in the Koran as the ruler that imprisons the people of Gog and Magog behind a wall of iron, while the famous Persian poet Nezami, in *Iskander-name*, makes the conqueror into a just and wise king inspired by God. The work of the Pseudo-Callisthenes enjoyed great fortune in the West during the Middle Ages, and its chivalrous protagonist, aside from being a champion of generosity, became a model for the troubadours and was sometimes presented as the bearer of Christian values, thus giving life to a large cycle of exploits that in the time came to rival those of Arthur and Charlemagne in popularity. Not all the medieval images of Alexander are positive, however. Church

Right: Alexander isolates twenty-two nations with copper gates: the subject of one of the 250 miniatures illustrating a fifteenth-century manuscript of *The Romance of Alexander* by the Pseudo-Callisthenes, from Crete or Cyprus; Museo delle Icone, Istituto Ellenico di Studi Bizantini e Post-Bizantini, Venice.

Left: Alexander consults the "Tree of the Moon" in a miniature from the *World Chronicle*, a thirteenth-century manuscript; University of Heidelberg.

Opposite: Miniature presenting Alexander and the seven sages, from the *Khamse* by Nezami (ca. 1590). In this Persian work, the king of the Macedonians is no longer a monarch and warrior, but is endowed with sacred virtues and is at the center of a discussion of worldly knowledge. According to Islamic tradition, each prophet had miraculous qualities: Alexander's was his knowledge of all the languages of the world.

Below: Alexander ascends in a basket drawn by griffons in a relief on the north wall of the Basilica of St. Mark, Venice.

was presented as such in works like the floor mosaics of the cathedrals of Trani and Otranto in southern Italy. Some Bible commentators, probably confusing him with other rulers of antiquity, went so far as to consider him a precursor of the Anti-Christ. Outside the church, the image of Alexander continued to adorn illuminated manuscripts and the walls of great halls, such as that of the castle of Mantua, where he appears in the company of the great rulers of antiquity. During the Renaissance, the events of his life provided subjects for artists such as Raphael, Sodoma, and Perin del Vaga. Later, he was made a protagonist in theatrical works by Racine and Metastasio. He was praised by such Enlightenment writers as Montesquieu and Voltaire and was chosen as an ideal model by Louis XIV and Napoleon, both of whom had their court artists create images of him. And today, long after the age of the great monarchs and even though works by recent historians have brought to light his human and political failings, the fame of this exceptional man and his "brief but glorious" life continue to awaken interest and curiosity.

authorities took a dim view of some of his exploits, especially his ascent into the sky, which was looked upon as a demonstration of demoniac pride and

Voltaire

"The only thing we can be sure of is that Alexander, at only twenty-four, had conquered Persia in three battles, that he was as brilliant as he was courageous, and that he changed the nature of Asia, Greece, and Egypt and gave new direction to the world."

Dictionary of Names and Places

Antigonus (Antigonus Cyclops) Macedonian general and ruler in Asia (382–301 BC). Collaborator of Philip II; during Alexander's expedition he commanded the Greek contingent and later controlled the satrapy of Phrygia. On Alexander's death, he took over the nearby satrapies and allied with Antipater and Craterus against Eumenes and Perdiccas to support the unity of the empire. In the civil wars that followed the death of Alexander, he took over the rule of Media, Syria, and Babylonia and took the title of king. Confronted by a coalition of the other Diadochi, he fought a long war that ended with his death in the battle of Ipsus. After further struggles, his son Demetrius Poliocretes became king of Macedonia, a title he handed on to his descendants.

Antipater Macedonian general (d. 319 BC). One of the most trusted lieutenants of Philip II, he maintained his position with the succession of Alexander, who named him regent of the state when he left for his expedition in Asia. He demonstrated great skill in that role, carrying out victorious campaigns against the Thracians and the Spartans of King Agis, thereby assuring Macedonian rule over Greece. Following Alexander's death he put down a new, large-scale rebellion led by the Athenians. Confirmed regent after the death of Perdiccas, of whom he had been an adversary, he held the position until his death, battling the more ambitious Diadochi. On the point of death, he named General Polyperchon as his successor, preferring him to his son Cassander.

Arachosia Satrapy of eastern Ariana, bordered on the north by the Hindu Kush and to the west by Drangiana and Aria, to the south by Gedrosia. Site of Alexandria Arachoton, today's Kandahar. Corresponds to contemporary southern Afghanistan (Registan and surrounding regions).

Aria Satrapy of eastern Ariana located at the westernmost end of the Hindu Kush. Bordered to the south by Arachosia and Drangiana, to the west by Parthia, and to the north by Margiana. Alexander founded Alexander Areion, today's Herat, in Aria. It corresponds to the contemporary territory of northwestern Afghanistan.

Ariana Geographic name during the Hellenistic period for the eastern provinces of the Persian Empire, the area between the Iranian plateau and the basins of the Oxus (Amu Darya) and Jaxartes (Syr Darya) rivers.

Aristander Lycian prophet. He was from Telmissus, site of a famous school of diviners, and he accompanied Alexander during the entire expedition, assisting him in the performance of sacrifices and proving himself always ready to interpret omens in a favorable light. The predictions he made on the eve of battle often served to encourage the troops.

Aristotle Greek philosopher (384–322 BC). Son of a doctor to Philip II, he began as a disciple in the school of Plato at Athens, remaining there until Plato's death. He then left Athens for Atarneus and Mytilene, where he dedicated himself to scientific research. Philip engaged him to oversee the education of Alexander, a role he performed for three years. He returned to Athens and founded a school in the Lyceum; because he lectured in the Lyceum's portico (*peripatos*) his school was given the name Peripatetic. Following Alexander's death he again left Athens and retired to Chalcis, on the island of Euboea, where he died. Aristotle's teaching influenced the entire course of the history of philosophy, from antiquity to the modern age. His primary contribution was a new concept of philosophic thought that no longer considered philosophy an exercise of knowledge or the use of ideas to improve the soul but as a scientific activity divided into separate disciplines for the analysis of all aspects of reality.

Arrhidaeus Macedonian king (d. 317 BC). Son of Philip II and his concubine Philinna, a Thessalian dancer. Mentally retarded—according to legend because of a potion prepared by Olympias—he seemed destined to have no role in political life, but following Alexander's death the assembled generals named him king of Macedonia with the name Philip III. Craterus was named to act as his custodian. After the death of Craterus, he fell into the hands of Olympias, who had him killed.

Artaxerxes III (Artaxerxes Ochus) King of Persia (d. 338 BC). Son of Artaxerxes II and thus cousin of the future Darius III. During much of his reign he had to face the continuous revolts of satraps. A cruel ruler, he devastated Syria and ravaged Sidon. He reconquered Egypt, which had won back its independence, driving out the last pharaoh, Nectanebo II. The eunuch Bagoas, who feared the loss of his authority at court, poisoned him.

Assaceni Central Asian mountain people inhabiting the region of Swat, in northern Pakistan, on the border with Kashmir.

Assyria Region between the mountains of Armenia, the westernmost end of the Zagros Mountains, and the Tigris River. It was the cradle of the ancient civilization of the Assyrians. The ancient Assyrian territory corresponds to an area between northern Iraq and eastern Turkey.

Attalus Macedonian general (d. 336 BC). Head of one of the most powerful clans in Macedonia and related to Philip II by way of marriage (Philip's wife Cleopatra was Attalus's niece). With Parmenion, he led the forces that established a bridgehead in Asia. On Philip's death he was killed by assassins sent by Alexander, who saw him as an obstacle to his power.

Bactria Satrapy of eastern Ariana, located between the mountains of Pamir and the eastern end of the Iranian plateau, crossed by the Oxus River. Bordered to the north by Sodgiana, to the south by Arachosia, and to the west by Aria and Margiana. It corresponds to the regions of Kabul and Mazar-i-Sharif in northern Afghanistan. Its capital, Bactra, is today's Balkh.

Barsine Favorite concubine of Alexander (356–309 BC?). Daughter of the satrap Artabazus, she was first the wife of Mentor and then of his brother Memnon, commanders of her father's mercenary troops. When Artabazus was defeated by Artaxerxes III, he took his family to Pella, where she may have met Alexander (she was about ten years older than him). Widowed, she was captured at Issus by Parmenion, who offered her to Alexander. Their relationship lasted roughly five years and resulted in the birth of Heracles, killed when still a child by Cassander.

Bessus Satrap of Bactria (d. 329 BC). Member of the Achaemenid dynasty and relative of Darius III. He took part in the battle of Gaugamela as commander of the Persian left wing. Following the defeat, he accompanied Darius to Ecbatana, but faced with Darius's obvious inability to stop the invaders he decided to depose him. He proclaimed himself successor to Darius under the name Artaxerxes V. Pursued by Alexander into the heart of central Asia, he was captured and killed.

Calanus Indian gymnosophist (literally "naked philosopher") (d. 324 BC). Having completed the thirty-seven years of ascetic life prescribed by tradition for religious Indians, he felt free to accompany Alexander and his army. According to biographers, he gave Alexander sage advice on several occasions. He survived the crossing of the Gedrosian desert, only to fall ill on his arrival in Persia. He decided to destroy his mortal remains by burning himself alive on a pyre, which he did in the presence of Alexander and the entire army, saluted (it is said) even by the elephants.

Callisthenes Greek historian (370–327 BC). Cousin of Aristotle, he accompanied the expedition to Asia, writing its chronicle. Until the fall of Darius III, he exalted the exploits of Alexander, celebrating him as a champion of the Greek world and contrasting him to the barbarous peoples of the Persian Empire. Callisthenes was unable to understand the enormous change in Alexander's political stance and openly found fault with the Orientalizing manners Alexander promoted. Having lost favor, he was accused of having instigated the Royal Pages' Conspiracy. He was arrested and probably died in prison. He was the author of a ten-volume history of Greece, of which only a few fragments remain. During the Middle Ages, he was believed to be the author of the highly popular *Romance of Alexander*, which instead was written much later.

Cambyses II King of Persia (d. 522 BC). Son and successor of Cyrus the Great, he strengthened and enlarged the Persian Empire, conquering Egypt. To gain full power, he killed his brother Smerdis. On his death, his throne was usurped by an impostor claiming to be Smerdis (this "false Smerdis" was actually a Magian priest named Gaumata).

Cappadocia Vast region of Asia Minor between Ionia and Armenia; it was the heart of the Hittite Empire. During the Achaemenid period, it was divided into two satrapies, Cappadocia and Pontic Cappadocia. The area is today within the area of Turkey.

Caria Satrapy of Asia Minor bordering Lydia and Phrygia to the north and Lycia to the south. The Ionian cities of Miletus and Halicarnassus were founded on the coast of Caria. The area is today part of Turkey.

Cassander Macedonian general (350–297 BC). Son of Antipater, he did not take part in the expedition to Asia. The same age as Alexander, he deeply resented him because Alexander had publicly humiliated him. Ferocious and cruel, he was excluded from the succession even by his father, who left the regency of the country to General Polyperchon. Cassander, however, went to war against his rival, defeated him, and proclaimed himself king of Macedonia, also eliminating all other members of the Argead dynasty. He held power in Greece for many years, leaving the kingdom to his son, Philip, who was dethroned by Demetrius Poliocretes.

Cleitus (Cleitus the Black) Macedonian general (d. 328 BC). Son of Alexander's wet nurse and boyhood friend of Alexander, whose life he saved at the battle of the Granicus. Commander of the royal squadron, the elite group of Shield Bearers, he gave proof of his great courage in all the major battles. As recompense for the services rendered, he was made satrap of Bactria, but never assumed the post. During a banquet at Maracanda he had an argument with Alexander in which he dared to criticize his conduct; Alexander, drunk and furious, killed him.

Coenus Macedonian general (d. 326 BC). A secondary commander until the plot in which Philotas and Parmenion (respectively his brother-in-law and father-in-law) were accused. Coenus was among the most pitiless accusers of Philotas, and his brother Cleander, vice commander of Parmenion, participated directly in the assassination of Parmenion. Coenus showed great valor in the expedition, distinguishing himself in the struggle against Spitamenes and in the battle of Hydaspes. He was spokesman for the army and convinced Alexander to halt his advance

to the Ganges. He died of an illness a few months later, near the Hydaspes River. Alexander honored him with a stately funeral.

Craterus Macedonian general (d. 321 BC). He took part in the expedition to Asia and was among Alexander's close friends. He is said to have saved Alexander's life during a lion hunt. Faithful to Alexander but also brutal and ambitious, he accused Philotas of treason and was among those who wanted him condemned to death. Following the murder of Parmenion, he became the vice-commander of the army. On the return from India, Alexander had him marry a niece of Darius III and made him regent of Macedonia in place of Antipater. He joined Antipater against Perdiccas and Eumenes in the struggle for the succession to Alexander. He was defeated by Eumenes and died in battle.

Cyrus the Great King of Persia, founder of the greatness of the Achaemenid dynasty (d. 529 BC). Son of an Iranian noble and a Median princess, at the death of his maternal grandfather, Astyages, he unified the dynasties of Persia and Media, forming a strong kingdom later enlarged with the conquest of Lydia and Mesopotamia. In order to govern this vast territory, Cyrus divided it into satrapies granted a certain amount of autonomy and showed much tolerance for the subject peoples. For these reasons Cyrus was looked upon, even by the Greeks, as the ideal ruler, wise and just, and so he appears in the *History* of Herodotus and the *Cyropaedia* by Xenophon.

Dardani Warlike Illyrian people inhabiting the northern borders of Macedonia, between the Axius (Vardares) and Morava rivers.

Darius I (Darius the Great) King of Persia (d. 486 BC). He restored the rule of the Achaemenids after the usurpation of Gaumata the Magian, who had pretended to be Smerdis, the brother of Cambyses. He then reorganized the empire, which under his rule reached its greatest expansion and was divided into twenty tributary satrapies; he also attempted to relocate the axis of his dominions westward. On the pretext of responding to the help furnished by Athens to rebellious Ionian cities, he sent an enormous army to conquer Greece; it was defeated at Marathon, forcing him to abandon the undertaking. He died while making preparations for a new expedition.

Darius III (Darius Codomannus) King of Persia (380–330 BC). Member of a secondary branch of the Achaemenid dynasty (he was the son of a brother of Artaxerxes II), he took the throne in 336 BC, following the poisoning of Artaxerxes III and his son by the powerful eunuch Bagoas. Already famous for courage shown in war against the rebellious Cadusi, Darius gave immediate proof of his determination, first eliminating Bagoas and then acting to rehabilitate the empire, compromised by years of internal struggle. His efforts were frustrated by the arrival of Alexander, who in a few years' time stole away nearly all of his empire. He fled to the eastern provinces and was deposed and later murdered in a plot led by his relative Bessus and the satraps Barsentes and Satibarzanes. His body was recovered by Alexander, who had him buried and assumed the role of his successor.

Demosthenes Athenian politician and orator (384–322 BC). Promoter of a return to the imperialistic policy of Athens, he called attention to the danger posed to Greek liberty by Philip II in a series of orations (the three *Philippics* and the three *Olynthiacs*). He convinced the Athenians to form an anti-Macedonian alliance with the Thebans. He participated in the battle of Chaeronea as a hoplite, after which he continued his political pressure. When Philip died, he urged the Athenians to take up arms, convinced that Alexander would not present a danger. Although the destruction of Thebes demonstrated the contrary, Demosthenes did not lose his influence, and his passionate political self-defense in the oration *On the Crown* had a extremely positive reception. Involved in the Harpalus scandal, he was forced into temporary exile, but following Alexander's death he returned to Athens and promoted a new revolt against Macedonian rule. After being defeated by Antipater he was forced to kill himself to escape the murderers sent by Antipater.

Diogenes Greek Cynic philosopher (c. 412–323 BC). Famous for his eccentric habits and his independence from authority. Diogenes promoted an ethical doctrine of rare forcefulness, based on the idea that the virtuous life is the simple life. In particular, he taught that virtue was to be achieved through spiritual and physical exercise and by discarding all material comforts. His revolutionary teachings influenced Stoic philosophy and, in some ways, Christian doctrine.

Drangiana Satrapy of Ariana, located between Gedrosia, Parthia, Aria, and Archosia. It was a fertile plateau surrounded by deserts. Today its land is divided between Iran and Afghanistan and corresponds roughly to the region of Seistan.

Epirus Region of northwest Greece, bordering Ilyria, Macedonia, and Thessaly. During the age of Philip and Alexander it was inhabited by several tribes of mixed Illyrian-Macedonian language and culture. The principal group was the Molossians; Alexander's mother, Olympias, was from the royal family of the Molossians.

Eumenes Secretary to Philip II and to Alexander (362–316 BC). During the expedition to Asia he compiled the *Ephemeris*, the royal diaries in which were noted all the dates of the campaign, thus becoming a fundamental source for all the future histories and biographies of Alexander. After Alexander's death, he was given control of Cappadocia and Paphlagonia. He joined Perdiccas in the defense of the legitimate heirs. He proved his diplomatic and military skills and for a time effectively blocked the ambitions of the Diadochi, but he was defeated by Antigonus, taken prisoner, and executed.

Gedrosia Satrapy of Ariana, located on the coast of the Arabian Sea. Almost completely covered by a sterile sandy desert, it extended from Carmania (eastern Iran) to the border of India. Its area is today Beluchistan, divided between Iran and Pakistan.

Harpalus Macedonian dignitary (d. 324 BC). Childhood friend of Alexander; although lame and unsuited for military life, he accompanied the expedition to Asia, and Alexander made him satrap and administrator of the royal treasury. While Alexander was in India, Harpalus made unscrupulous use of the empire's funds. When Alexander returned, Harpalus fled to Athens with his personal army along with a large portion of the treasury. When Alexander requested his extradition, Harpalus managed to convince Demosthenes and other Athenian politicians to provide him with a means of escape. He took refuge on Crete and was assassinated by one of his own officers.

Hephaistion Macedonian general (d. 324 BC). The same age as Alexander, from childhood he was Alexander's closest friend. In the course of the expedition to Asia he performed various important roles, fighting courageously and enthusiastically supporting Alexander in his policy of equality between conquerors and conquered. His intimacy with Alexander was such that when Darius's mother saw him and, because of his majestic appearance, mistook him for Alexander, Alexander was not upset and instead declared, "He too is an Alexander." The affection between the two men never waned over the years and was celebrated in a series of official recognitions. During the wedding celebrations at Susa, Alexander made Hephaistion his brother-in-law by having him marry a daughter of Darius III; a little later, he named him chiliarch, the second most powerful position in the kingdom. Hephaistion occupied the position only a few months, dying suddenly that same year. The distraught Alexander had him paid semidivine honors. As long as Alexander was alive, the post of chiliarch was not given to anyone else.

Hermeias Greek politician (d. 341 BC). Born a slave, he was freed by the tyrant of Atarneus and attended the Platonic academy at Athens. He returned to Asia Minor and became the ruler of his birthplace but proved wise and just. His daughter married Aristotle, and he tried to form an anti-Persian alliance with Philip II. Betrayed, he was captured and tortured at length but refused to betray his accomplices and was executed.

Hyrcania Satrapy of northern Ariana, located between Media, Margiana, and the Caspian Sea. Its area corresponds to the region of the Mazandaran, near the modern-day city of Teheran (ancient Rhagae) in northern Iran.

Ichthyophagi (literally "fish-eaters"). Primitive inhabitants of the Makran, the coastal region of Gedrosia. They lived in miserable conditions, hardly changed from the Stone Age, raising sheep and eating the carcasses of beached whales, the bones of which they used to make utensils and shelters.

Illyrians Indo-European people related to the Thracians and divided in various tribes. The Illyrians gave their name to Illyria, the mountainous region of the Balkans facing the Adriatic, roughly corresponding to today's Albania and Montenegro.
Ionia Coastal region of western Anatolia, colonized by the Ionians and other Greek peoples, who founded important cities there, including Ephesus, Samos, and Miletus. It was a center of the clash between the Greek and Persian cultures. Ionia's rebellion against Achaemenid rule was the original cause of the Persian War.

Leonidas Epirot courtier and relative of Olympias. He was Alexander's first teacher and sought to inure him to the hardships of a soldier's life. When Alexander became king he gently chided Leonidas for his austerity, sending him a large quantity of myrrh and frankincense so that he would "not be stingy with the gods" when performing rites.

Lydia Satrapy of Asia Minor, located to the west of Phrygia and to the north of Caria. It rose to become a great power under its last ruler, King Croesus, but when he was defeated (ca. 546 BC) by Cyrus the Great, it was absorbed into the Persian Empire, its capital, Sardis, becoming one of the empire's major centers. Its area is today part of Turkey.

Lysimachus Macedonian general (360–281 BC). In the campaign in Asia, he proved himself one of the most capable commanders. Following Alexander's death, he was one of the Diadochi and obtained Thrace and surrounding territories. Over the course of the struggles among the successors of Alexander, he occupied for a certain period part of Asia Minor, Macedonia, and Thessaly. He died in the battle of Corupedion, confronted by Seleucus and Ptolemy.

Lysimachus Greek teacher. He narrated the exploits of the ancient Homeric heroes to Alexander, enormously influencing the character of the future conqueror. Although already advanced in years at the time of the expedition to Asia, he accompanied his former pupil and took part in military actions. On one occasion, in Phoenicia, the elder teacher was surrounded by an enemy detachment and Alexander risked his life to save him.

Malloi Warlike people of India, located in the region of the upper course of the Hyphasis (Beas) and Acesines (Chenab) rivers, tributaries of the Indus in modern-day Pakistan.

Mazaeus Persian politician. A figure of great authority, he was supreme satrap of Phoenicia, Cilicia, Syria, and Mesopotamia. After the battle of Gaugamela, in which he commanded the right wing of the army of Darius III, he handed over Babylon to Alexander without a struggle and joined Alexander. From then on, Mazaeus and his family occupied positions of great prestige at Alexander's court.

Media Mountainous region to the southwest of the Caspian Sea, bordering Armenia, Parthia, and Carmania. It was the center of the powerful Medean Empire, later subjected by the Persians. Its area is today inside western Iran.

Memnon (Memnon of Rhodes) Greek general (380–333 BC). He served the satrap Artabazus, father of Barsine, in a rebellion against Artaxerxes III. Defeated, he took refuge at Pella with Philip III, at whose court he probably met the infant Alexander. He returned to Asia, went into the service of Darius III, and defeated the expeditionary force led by Attalus and Parmenion. He participated in a secondary role in the battle of the Granicus and was made supreme commander of the defense of Asia Minor, which he conducted with great strategic skill, carrying out daring offensive operations in the Aegean. His sudden death, under the walls of Mytilene, freed Alexander from a powerful adversary.

Nearchus Macedonian admiral (d. 312 BC). Native of Crete, he was among Alexander's oldest friends and was among those condemned to exile following the Pixodarus affair. Early in the expedition to Asia, he was named satrap of Lycia, but he left that post for the campaign in India for Alexander had great trust in his gifts as a navigator and scientist. On the return journey, he commanded the fleet that sailed from the mouth of the Indus to that of the Tigris. This extraordinary undertaking won him the position of admiral in the planned expedition to conquer Arabia. At the death of Alexander, Nearchus put himself at the disposal of Antigonus and his son Demetrius. During his last years he lived apart, dedicating himself to the compilation of a report of his trip in the Persian Gulf, known today from its mention in other sources, primarily Arrian. Nearchus died at the battle of Gaza in the struggle against Ptolemy.

Nectanebo II Egyptian pharaoh (d. 343 BC). Last ruler of the thirtieth dynasty, he fought to defend Egypt from the Persian forces of Artaxerxes III. Defeated, he resisted a while longer in southern Egypt before disappearing into the Nubian Desert. In the legendary *Romance of Alexander,* Nectanebo is presented as a sorcerer who uses magic arts to seduce Olympias so that he can father Alexander.

Nysa Greek name for the tribes of mountain peoples living in the Chitral region of Pakistan. For various reasons, but most of all because of the presence in that area of grapes and ivy, the Greeks took them for the descendants of the companions of the god Dionysus. According to several modern scholars, they were the ancestors of the Kafirs.

Olympias Queen of Macedonia and mother of Alexander (375–316 BC). Daughter of Neoptolemus, king of Epirus, she married Philip II, with whom she had two children, Alexander and Cleopatra, who married her uncle, Alexander of Epirus. On the death of Philip II, Alexander, although nurturing strong affection for her, excluded her from the government, making Antipater his regent in Macedonia. During the difficult times following Alexander's death, the indomitable queen was an active participant in the struggles for the succession, supporting Polyperchon against Cassander and having Alexander's half-brother Arrhidaeus killed, along with many other adversaries. With the defeat of Polyperchon, she took refuge with his supporters in the coastal city of Pydna, which was then besieged by Cassander. She fell into the hands of her enemy and was handed over to the relatives of those she had killed, who executed her.

Onesicritus Greek philosopher and historian. Pupil of the Cynic philosopher Diogenes, he accompanied the Macedonian army during the campaign in India and was sent by Alexander to interrogate the local wise men. Nearchus had a high opinion of his abilities as a sailor and during the return journey appointed him helmsman of the fleet. Following

Alexander's death, Onesicritus retired to write a famous biography of the conqueror, of which only a few fragments remain.

Paeonians Tribe living to the north of Macedonia. Defeated by Philip II and Alexander, they were obliged to send contingents of soldiers to fight in the Macedonian army.

Parmenion Macedonian general (400–330 BC). He was Philip II's primary supporter, and together with Attalus, he led the expeditionary force to Asia. Following Philip's death, he became second-in-command to Alexander, making decisive contributions to the victories on the Granicus, Issus, and Gaugamela. He was put in command of the troops left behind at Ecbatana and—probably falsely—was believed to be involved in the plot for which his son Philotas was executed. Alexander sent murderers who betrayed and killed the elderly general in the garden of his palace.

Pausanias Macedonian official (d. 336 BC). He has entered history for having killed Alexander's father, Philip II. According to some biographers, he had been Philip's lover and had grown jealous at seeing himself replaced by another youth, a relative of Attalus. Attalus had invited Pausanias to dinner, got him drunk, and then had him raped by his servants. Turning to Philip for justice, Pausanias and was further disappointed when Philip refused to turn against Attalus and limited himself to making Pausanias a bodyguard. The embittered Pausanias decided to kill the ruler and was in turn killed while fleeing. According to another tradition, Pausanius had killed Philip on orders from Olyimpias, who later honored his memory.

Perdiccas Macedonian general (d. 321 BC). He took part valorously in all Alexander's exploits, distinguishing himself in the assault on Thebes and the battle of Gaugamela. The dying Alexander entrusted him with the royal ring and seal, but the other generals questioned his authority and allied against him. Proclaiming himself a supporter of the legitimate heir, Alexander IV, Perdiccas assumed the title of chiliarch and struggled to maintain the unity of the empire. In his final attempt to get the Diadochi to join him, he made himself the leader of various satrapies, but that only accelerated the dissolution of the state. He decided to use force to stop Ptolemy, who wanted to rule independently, and marched on Egypt, but was killed by several of his own officers in the course of a mutiny.

Persia Satrapy of western Ariana, located between the Persian Gulf, Carmania, and Media. It was the cradle of the Persian civilization and place of origin of the Achaemenid dynasty. The principal cities were the capital, Persepolis, located near today's Shiraz, and Pasargadae, site of the burial of the first Great Kings. The ancient territory corresponds to today's central-southern Iran.

Philip II King of Macedonia (382–336 BC). Youngest son of Amyntas III, he ascended the throne on the death of his older brothers, pushing aside his nephew Amyntas IV. After organizing a powerful army, he subdued the barbarous northern peoples (Illyrians, Thracians, and Paeonians) and took control of several cities allied to Athens and the rich mines of Mount Pangaeus. Having strengthened and enlarged the borders of the kingdom, he directed his attention to the south. His triumphs over Pherae, the ruling city of Thessaly, and Phocis demonstrated that he was a major power. This awakened the fears of the Thebans and Athenians, who allied against him. Breaking their resistance at Chaeronea, Philip forced the creation of the League of Corinth, which he then had nominate him commander of an expedition against the Persian Empire. On the eve of his departure, he was assassinated by Pausanias, one of his bodyguards.

Philotas Macedonian general (d. 330 BC). Son of Parmenion, he was one of the oldest companions of Alexander, although he may have betrayed his trust during the Pixodarus affair. In fact, it was probably Philotas who revealed to Philip that Alexander had interfered in the marriage negotiations with the satrap. During the expedition to Asia he commanded the cavalry and gave repeated proof of his courage. Daring and proud, he did not hesitate to criticize the Orientalizing manners that Alexander introduced, thus attracting the anger of Alexander, who eventually saw him as a dangerous opponent. Accused, whether rightly or wrongly, of having participated in a plot against Alexander, he was arrested, tortured, and executed by his own soldiers, who acted on instructions from Alexander.

Phoenicia Maritime region of the Syrian-Palestinian area inhabited by Phoenicians, a branch of the Canaanites. It was divided into several independent city-states, the most famous of which were Aradus, Heliopolis, Byblos, Sidon, and Tyre. It was the site of one of the most important civilizations of the Mediterranean.

Phrygia Region that included the western area of the Anatolian plain. Inhabited by the ancient population of the Phrygians, from Macedonia; its capital city was Gordium, named for its legendary founder, Gordius. The area that was Phrygia is today part of Turkey.

Pixodarus Satrap of Caria. Brother of Mausolus, who had ruled as an independent sovereign. Pixodarus became his successor by pushing aside his older sister, Ada, with the help of the Persians. In an attempt to achieve independence, he conducted secret negotiations with Philip II, proposing a marriage between Arrhidaeus and his daughter. The negotiations failed because of the interference of Alexander, who proposed himself in the place of his half-brother, awakening the anger of Philip. The frightened Pixodarus then rushed to proclaim his devotion to the Great King. On the death of Pixodarus the satrapy passed into the hands of a Persian general, but Alexander put Ada back on the throne.

Porus Indian rajah (370–317 BC). Ruler of Paurava, he reigned over the region between the rivers Hydaspes (today's Jhelum) and Acesines (Chenab). Defeated and taken prisoner at the battle of Hydaspes, he submitted to Alexander and became his most faithful ally in the region. In that role he tried to convince Alexander to continue his campaign into the heart of India, convinced that their combined forces could easily have overturned the empire of Ksandrames, king of Magadha and ruler of the entire Ganges plain. The undertaking was prevented by the mutiny of Alexander's soldiers. After Alexander's death, Porus came into conflict with the Macedonian satrap of India, Eudamus, who killed him to get his war elephants.

Ptolemy Macedonian general (367–286 BC). A few years younger than Alexander, he participated in the expedition to Asia, distinguishing himself during the campaign in India. After Alexander's death, he was named satrap of Egypt, which he soon transformed into an independent kingdom. Threatened by Perdiccas and the other Diadochi, he became involved in a long struggle, in the course of which he enlarged and consolidated his dominion. Ptolemy made an important contribution to world culture by founding the great library at Alexandria. He wrote a history of Alexander's exploits, but it was unfortunately lost. At his death, the kingdom passed to his descendants, the last of whom was the famous Cleopatra.

Roxane Persian noble (d. 310 BC). Taken prisoner in Bactria together with her father, Oxyartes, she was married by Alexander who hoped to thereby indicate his intention to give equal standing to Macedonians and Persians. When Alexander died, Roxane was pregnant with a child that was later named Alexander. She became involved in the wars among the Diadochi and in the hope of ensuring the success of her son approached first Perdiccas, then Antipater, and finally Oympias. Following the deaths of all her protectors, she was captured by Cassander and killed together with her son in the fortress of Amphipolis.

Samaria Territory in Palestine, located to the west of the Jordan. Following a rebellion against Alexander, its inhabitants were punished with a cruel massacre and with the destruction of the capital, Samaria, on the ruins of which rose a Macedonian settlement.

Seleucus I (Seleucus Nicator) King of Syria, general of Alexander (358–281 BC). He took part in the campaign in India and at the death of Alexander was among the leaders in the struggles among the Diadochi. Made satrap of Babylonia, he was driven out by Antigonus and took refuge in Egypt. With the defeat of his rival he reoccupied Mesopotamia, adding Media and much of Ariana to his territory. After defeating Lysimachus, he unified a vast area of Alexander's empire, between the Hellespont and the Indus, and revived Alexander's dream of the ethnic fusion of the empire. He was killed while trying to occupy Macedonia. His descendants, the Seleucids, reigned until the Roman epoch.

Sisygambis Persian noble (d. 323 BC). Wife of Arsames, brother of Artaxerxes II, mother of Darius

III, Oxyathres, and Stateira. Taken prisoner after the battle of Issus, she was highly honored by Alexander, who made certain she was given the treatment her rank deserved. After Alexander's death she starved herself to death, in that way demonstrating her devotion to the man who had treated her with such dignity.

Sogdiana Satrapy of eastern Ariana, bounded by the Jaxartes River to the north and by the Oxus to the south. On its territory Alexander founded Alexandria on Oxus, Alexandria-in-Sogdia (Ali Khanum), and on its northern border, Alexandria-the-Farthest (Khojend). The territory of this ancient region is today divided among Uzbekistan, Tajikistan, and Kyrgyzstan.

Spitamenes Persian noble (d. 328 BC). He supported Bessus in the struggle against Alexander, and at the death of Bessus took command of the rebels, leading a series of surprise attacks against Macedonian garrisons. He succeeded in annihilating a Macedonian column but was then defeated by the Macedonians and betrayed by his Scythian allies, who cut off his head. His daughter Apame married Seleucus, one of the Diadochi, thus becoming progenitor of a dynasty of Hellenistic rulers.

Stateira Persian princess (d. 323 BC). Eldest daughter of Darius III and his sister and wife Stateira. Taken prisoner by the Macedonians after the battle of Issus, she was offered to Alexander during the siege of Tyre. He refused, but a few years later, at the end of the Indian campaign, he changed his mind. By then Alexander believed that intermarrying with the Iranian nobility was an ideal way to consolidate the empire. He thus decided to marry both Stateira and the youngest daughter of Artaxerxes III. These were brief unions, however, since Alexander died a little later, and Roxane, eager to rid herself of rivals, had both women killed with the complicity of Perdiccas.

Taulanti Tribe of ferocious warriors, related to the Illyrians, located to the northwest of Macedonia.

Thais Athenian courtesan. Considered the instigator of the fire in the royal palace of Persepolis, she later became the mistress of Ptolemy, giving him three children. Dante speaks of her unsympathetically in the *Inferno*.

Thessaly Region of continental Greece located to the south of Mount Olympus, bordering Macedonia to the north and Epirus to the west. Famed horsemen, the Thessalians were among the most valiant allies of both Philip and Alexander in their campaigns.

Thracians Indo-European population, probably related to the Illyrians, inhabitants from remote antiquity of the central area of the Balkan peninsula, a territory today divided among Greece, Turkey, and Bulgaria. Violent and primitive, the Thracians were subdued by Philip and later again by Alexander, to whom they furnished a contingent that took part in the campaign in Asia.

Triballians Thracian tribe of the fourth century BC in the region at the mouth of the Ister (Danube), defeated by Alexander.

Xerxes I (Xerxes the Great; Ahasuerus) King of Persia (d. 465 BC). Son of Darius I, he continued his father's plan to subdue Greece. To that end, he assembled a large expedition that broke the Greek resistance at Thermopylae and reached Athens. The Persian fleet was then destroyed at Salamis, under the eyes of Xerxes, who watched the battle from a throne erected on a nearby hill. On his return home, he learned that his army had also been destroyed. The story of Xerxes' invasion is the subject of the tragedy *The Persians*, by Aeschylus.

Bibliography

Ancient sources:

Arrian. *The Campaigns of Alexander*. Penguin Books, 1982.

Diodorus Siculus. *Library of History*, Books XVI–XL, Loeb Classical Library, 1983.

Justin. *Epitome of the Philippic History of Pompeius Trogus*. Claredon Press, Oxford, 1997.

Plutarch. *The Age of Alexander*. Penguin Books, 1988.

Plutarch. *Plutarch's Lives*. The Modern Library, 1992.

Pseudo-Callisthenes. *The Greek Alexander Romance*. Penguin Books, 1991.

Quintus Curtius Rufus. *The History of Alexander*. Penguin Books, 1984.

Strabo. *Geography, II Caucasus and Asia Minor*. Harvard University Press, 1988–97.

Books on Alexander:

Bosworth, A. B. *Conquest and Empire: The Reign of Alexander the Great*. Cambridge: Cambridge University Press, 1988.

Briant, Pierre. *Alexander the Great*. London: Thames and Hudson, 1996.

Engels, D. W. *Alexander the Great and the Logistics of the Macedonian Army*. Berkeley, Los Angeles, London: University of California Press, 1978.

Green, Peter. *Alexander the Great*. New York: Praeger, 1970.

------. *Alexander of Macedon, 356–323 BC: A Historical Biography*. Berkeley, Los Angeles, London: University of California Press, 1991.

Hammond, N. G. L. *Alexander the Great: King, Commander, and Statesman*. Bristol: The Bristol Press, 1994.

------. *The Genius of Alexander the Great*. London: Duckworth, 1997.

Lane Fox, Robin. *Alexander the Great*. London: Allen Lane, 1973.

------. *The Search for Alexander the Great*. New York: Little, Brown, 1980.

Milns, R. D. *Alexander the Great*. London: Hale, 1968.

O'Brian, John Maxwell. *Alexander the Great: The Invisible Enemy. A Biography*. London–New York, Routledge, 1992.

Rice, E. E. *Alexander the Great*. Gloucestershire: Sutton Publishing, 1997.

Tarn, W. W. *Alexander the Great*. Cambridge: Cambridge University Press, 1948.

Photographic References

Archivio Alinari, Florence
Archivio Electa, Milan
Artothek, Weilheim
Bildarchiv Preu
ßischer Kulturbesitz, Berlin
Cameraphoto, Venice
Giraudon/Archivio Alinari, Florence
Grazia Neri, Milan
Réunione des Musées Nationaux, Paris

Thanks to all the archives and museums that have
kindly made photographic material available.